Contents

Chapter 1: Social media and us

What is social media and how did it grow so quickly?   1

How the UK uses social media   3

A decade of digital dependency   4

The average person has seven social media accounts   6

So long social media: the kids are opting out of the online public square   7

Why did you use social media today?   10

Young people spend a third of their leisure time on devices   11

Teenagers shun homework for social media and video games   12

My generation's dark addiction to social media   13

Facebook to launch 'take a break' pop-up warnings to help children spend less time on social media   14

'Fear of missing out' driving social media addiction, study suggests   15

Social media is as harmful as alcohol and drugs for millennials   16

Teenagers are getting plastic surgery to look like their snapchat selfies   17

Admit it, older people – you are addicted to your phones, too   18

Digital addiction: how technology keeps us hooked   19

Chapter 2: Safer networking

Safer Internet Day 2018 – a parent's perspective   20

The view of young people on social media   22

How a Digital 5 A Day can help children lead healthy online lives   23

Young people and social networking services   24

#StatusOfMind   25

Digital footprints   27

What information shouldn't you post on social media?   28

How can we stop social media undermining our mental health?   29

Social media bad for mental health? Not in my view!   30

A 'Goldilocks amount of screen time' might be good for teenagers' well-being   31

What is cyberbullying?   32

What to do if you're being bullied on a social network   33

Chapter 3: Digital detox

Scroll Free September aims to wean us off social media   36

Social media users are being encouraged to cut out some of their favourite platforms for 'Scroll Free September'   37

Social media: six steps to take back control   38

Break away from phone addiction with this simple trick   39

Key facts   40

Glossary   41

Assignments   42

Index   43

Acknowledgements   44

Introduction

SOCIAL NETWORKING is Volume 340 in the **ISSUES** series. The aim of the series is to offer current, diverse information about important issues in our world, from a UK perspective.

ABOUT SOCIAL NETWORKING

Social networking has seen a massive rise in a relatively short period of time. It is constantly evolving and transforming the way we live our lives. Social media is used, on average by 99% of 16–24-year-olds and for about an hour every day. This book explores the rise of social media sites and how to use them safely.

OUR SOURCES

Titles in the **ISSUES** series are designed to function as educational resource books, providing a balanced overview of a specific subject.

The information in our books is comprised of facts, articles and opinions from many different sources, including:

⇨ Newspaper reports and opinion pieces

⇨ Website factsheets

⇨ Magazine and journal articles

⇨ Statistics and surveys

⇨ Government reports

⇨ Literature from special interest groups.

A NOTE ON CRITICAL EVALUATION

Because the information reprinted here is from a number of different sources, readers should bear in mind the origin of the text and whether the source is likely to have a particular bias when presenting information (or when conducting their research). It is hoped that, as you read about the many aspects of the issues explored in this book, you will critically evaluate the information presented.

It is important that you decide whether you are being presented with facts or opinions. Does the writer give a biased or unbiased report? If an opinion is being expressed, do you agree with the writer? Is there potential bias to the 'facts' or statistics behind an article?

ASSIGNMENTS

In the back of this book, you will find a selection of assignments designed to help you engage with the articles you have been reading and to explore your own opinions. Some tasks will take longer than others and there is a mixture of design, writing and research-based activities that you can complete alone or in a group.

Useful weblinks

www.bcs.org

www.bullying.co.uk

www.childnet.com

www.childrenscommissioner.gov.uk

www.familylives.org.uk

www.independent.co.uk

www.inews.co.uk

www.marketingtechnews.net

www.mentalhealth.org.uk

www.ntu.ac.uk

www.ofcom.org.uk

www.ons.gov.uk

www.ox.ac.uk

www.rethink.org

www.rsph.org.uk

www.shoutoutuk.org

www.telegraph.co.uk

www.theconversation.com

www.theguardian.com

www.ucl.ac.uk

www.uk.kantar.com

www.wlv.ac.uk

FURTHER RESEARCH

At the end of each article we have listed its source and a website that you can visit if you would like to conduct your own research. Please remember to critically evaluate any sources that you consult and consider whether the information you are viewing is accurate and unbiased.

Social Networking

Editor: Tina Brand

Volume 340

Independence Educational Publishers

First published by Independence Educational Publishers

The Studio, High Green

Great Shelford

Cambridge CB22 5EG

England

© Independence 2018

ISBN–13: 978 1 86168 791 3

Printed in Great Britain

Zenith Print Group

What is social media and how did it grow so quickly?

By James Carson

You're more likely than not to have used social media recently, and it's also likely that the time you've spent on the platforms has clocked up at least several hours a month. For instance, 99 per cent of people aged 16–24 in the UK in 2016 said they had used social media within the past week, while they spent close to an hour a day using it to communicate.

The popular social media platforms are obvious to most people – Facebook has a UK audience of some 40 million, LinkedIn and Twitter both exceed 20 million, and Instagram, Pinterest and Snapchat have close to ten million each. The reach of these platforms makes it clear that social media is now ubiquitous. But for all the big name players, what is the definition of social media? Where did it come from? And how did it gain such an important role in our lives so quickly?

What is social media?

If we take the words 'social media' at their basic level, it is media that allows people to connect with each other. Email allows you to connect and interact with other people, so it is 'social'. But given most email is just text-based messaging and delivered and received on a one-to-one basis, it's a communication tool rather than media.

The Oxford Living Dictionaries website defines it as 'Websites and applications to create and share content or to participate in social networking'. Facebook, LinkedIn and Twitter fit neatly within this definition.

All of these sites allow users to create and share content with an audience – the essential media element that email is missing. On all sites, there are methods of connection and building a network: Facebook friends, followers on Twitter and connections on LinkedIn. In many cases, you will not have met all of these connections in real life (although that is less true in the case of Facebook friends), so followers can often represent more of an 'audience' than being actual collaborators.

Social media is also closely associated with 'Web 2.0' – the concept of the 'second stage' of the web popularised by Tim O'Reilly and Dale Dougherty. In the first stage of the web, users were limited to passive viewing of content; for example, they would go to a website and be able to access its information, but not be able to interact with it.

With Web 2.0, the Internet is thought of as a platform in itself, where people are essentially building applications within it. The more people collaborating, the better the applications get, and where users are able to interact with the content and create their own.

Where did social media come from?

While interactive chat rooms stretch back to before the World Wide Web, social networking as we understand it today really began to evolve in the late 1990s with the launch of multiple instant messaging services. For instance, both MSN Messenger and Yahoo! Messenger, along with their Internet chat rooms, both launched in 1999.

Instant messaging isn't comfortably defined as social media, because, similar to email, it's mostly text based and is more of a one-to-one communication tool, although you could participate in small groups. However, messaging is a crucial element of many social networking services today and an important precursor.

The real 'Web 2.0' social media, where users could upload and share content, along with networking with other people, began a few years later.

How did social media grow so quickly?

It was really advances in web publishing technology and the idea of inverting access to publishing tools from backend Content Management Systems (CMS) to front-end users that first enabled social media. But there are four other crucial points in its history that led to it becoming ubiquitous.

1. Broadband

Do you remember trying to look at images on a web browser using a 56 k/b dial-up connection? In the 1990s, this activity was painfully slow – often prohibitively, and not helped by a lot of the web not adhering to usability standards that we see as the norm today.

Downloading a low-quality film of around 700 MB would take three to five days. The creation of broadband infrastructure that began in the early 2000s was the first important step in allowing social media. Faster download and upload times meant that people could download and upload from the new social media tools much more quickly.

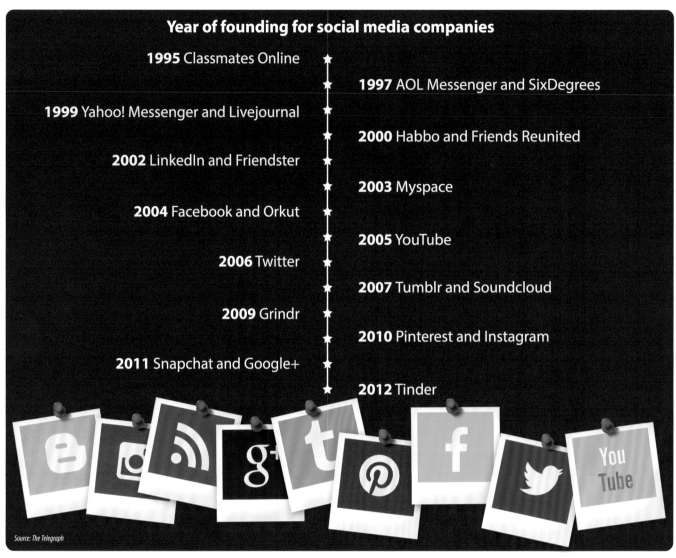

Year of founding for social media companies

- **1995** Classmates Online
- **1997** AOL Messenger and SixDegrees
- **1999** Yahoo! Messenger and Livejournal
- **2000** Habbo and Friends Reunited
- **2002** LinkedIn and Friendster
- **2003** Myspace
- **2004** Facebook and Orkut
- **2005** YouTube
- **2006** Twitter
- **2007** Tumblr and Soundcloud
- **2009** Grindr
- **2010** Pinterest and Instagram
- **2011** Snapchat and Google+
- **2012** Tinder

Source: The Telegraph

2. Cloud computing

In his book *Thank You For Being Late: An Optimist's Guide to Thriving in the Age of Accelerations,* Thomas L Friedman says 2007 as being one of the seminal years in Internet technology. The Kindle was launched, Google introduced Android, Steve Jobs unveiled the first iPhone, AirBnb was conceived to name a few.

Perhaps most importantly was the launch of Hadoop, which enabled the mass storage and analysis of unstructured data. This led to cloud computing, which is one of the key reasons why social networks can store such vast quantities of data.

3. Mobile Internet

The smartphone became a widely owned product around 2009–2010. Previously, people could only access social media from desktops, which limited their time spent and possible interactions.

With the advent of fully functioning web mobile web browsers, native social media applications, and WiFi and mobile data networks, it was possible to be on social media at almost any time if you wanted to be.

4: In-built 'virality'

A classic story of the early Internet is how the creators of Hotmail were told by an investor to automatically sign off every email with 'Get your free email at HoTMaiL' and a link back to their homepage. As people received Hotmail emails, they were tempted to sign up to the service because of the message, and the popularity of the service exploded.

One of YouTube's great viral marketing ploys was to allow anyone to embed the videos on their own website. YouTube embeds soon became a feature of many articles.

Both of these are examples of in-built 'virality' – the content within the services may be viral (like chain emails or viral videos being passed on by email) but also the way the networks themselves expanded was viral.

Services like Twitter and Facebook asked new sign ups to email friends on their email lists to get them to join, suggesting the experience will be better if you do. Once signed up, users tend to receive a lot of email notifications from the platforms about almost every interaction (unless you turn them off). The networks are then gamified through the enticement to gain likes, retweets or followers. This keeps people going back and sticking to the network.

31 July 2017

How the UK uses social media

By Kirsty Cooke

To celebrate Social Media Day (30 June 2018), we've gathered some of the top insights from across Kantar on how the UK is engaging with social channels…

Barely a day passes when the marketing press doesn't mention the importance of social media – how brands can reach new audiences, take advantage of social commerce, engage consumers and even build their brands through these channels.

As tomorrow is Social Media Day, let's take a look at what British consumers are actually doing on Facebook, Twitter and Instagram, and what brands can do to capitalise on this behaviour…

63% of the UK uses social media every single day

According to Connected Life from Kantar TNS, 77% of the UK are accessing social networks each week; 4.8 different platforms are used on a weekly basis. The range of networks used is often much smaller than that of other countries, partially explained by the fact that there are no established local networks, so global giants dominate (especially amongst those in older age groups).

Perhaps unsurprisingly, younger people are more active on social media

Kantar research reveals that around 22% of daily mobile phone usage amongst those under 21 is spent with social media. Out of the three hours per day centennials spend on their phones, 11 mins is allocated to Facebook, just five to Twitter and 13.65 to Snapchat. (31.95 minutes are spent on YouTube, on average.) Those over 21 spend less time on their phones (2.4 hours a day) and prefer Facebook, spending nearly 15 minutes on this channel per day. The Kantar Millward Brown *AdReaction: engaging Gen X, Y and Z* shows that Gen Z (16–19-year-olds) also demand far greater control over ad exposure but appreciate opportunities to interact with ads e.g. via voting. They particularly like ads with humour, which is the most important characteristic of good branded content according to the research.

Young people are also most easily 'influenced'

More and more brands are using celebrities or influencers as a way of reaching consumers, and the Kantar Millward Brown *AdReaction* study in 2017 showed that Gen Z are significantly more receptive than other generations to content featuring celebrities and social media celebrities, and results show ads with a celebrity presence result in a 16% greater impact on brand awareness than those without. Of course, brands need to be mindful of actually building long-term partnerships with influencers, and picking spokespeople who are relevant for the brand.

The UK loves Tweeting about telly

In 2017, over 130 million TV-related tweets were sent from 4.2 million unique authors, accounting for just over 7% of UK TV viewers. (Social TV Tools KSTR, Kantar Media. Twitter data is from tweets tracked or defined as TV related tweets during 2017.)

63% of people say they like to read other people's views and opinions online

Data from Kantar Media's *TGI Clickstream study Q2 2018* shows the value of 'user-generated content', with a further 57% agreeing that 'people's online opinions help me make decisions about major purchases.'

People do actually respond well to adverts on social channels

Kantar Millward Brown's *Social Media: Deal or no Deal?* study demonstrates that overall, the news is positive for advertising on social media (specifically Facebook and Instagram). The analysis proves that there is a positive impact on brand building as well as sales. However, brands must adapt to social environments in order to succeed: brands that use language that is more 'human' have better engagement with consumers, the research showed.

BUT half of us aren't really seeing what we want from brands:

50% of the UK (compared to 32% globally) say: 'Overall, the things brands post on social media are not relevant to me.' (Kantar TNS *Connected Life 2017*). And when asked what posts irritated them most on social media channels in a Lightspeed survey, 46% said 'ads you have to click past' and 41% said 'ads that automatically play sound'.

Just 30% of the UK trust social media as a news source

Kantar's *Trust in News* study found that the supposed rise of 'fake news' actually improved the perceived credibility of traditional news sources, such as printed newspapers (trust levels in the UK of 57.5%) and news magazines (65.6%) and TV news (70%). 58% of respondents said they now had LOWER trust in social media as a news source than they had previously; just 8% said they trusted it more (following hearing about 'fake news'). And according to a Lightspeed survey, the worst type of post on social media (at 56%)? Fake news.

BUT people still get their news from social channels

47% of UK adults say they often find out about breaking news and events through social networking sites first. (Kantar Media's *TGI Clickstream study Q2 2018*.) Of course, many will fact check the news somewhere else to verify it – over 75% (globally) according to the *Trust in News* study – but 15% will share a story after reading only the headline. Sigh.

29 June 2018

⇨ The above information is reprinted with kind permission from Kantar UK. Please visit www.kantar.com for further information.

A decade of digital dependency

Most people in the UK are dependent on their digital devices and need a constant connection to the Internet, according to research published today by Ofcom.

Ofcom's *Communications Market Report* is our most comprehensive study of how communications services in the UK are changing. This year it focuses on how technology has revolutionised our lives over the past ten years.

2008 was the year the smartphone took off in the UK. With the iPhone and Android fresh into the UK market, 17% of people owned a smartphone a decade ago. That has now reached 78%, and 95% among 16–24-year-olds. The smartphone is now the device people say they would miss the most, dominating many people's lives in both positive and negative ways.

People in the UK now check their smartphones, on average, every 12 minutes of the waking day. Two in five adults (40%) first look at their phone within five minutes of waking up, climbing to 65% of those aged under 35. Similarly, 37% of adults check their phones five minutes before lights out, again rising to 60% of under-35s.

Always on

In contrast to a decade ago, most people now say they need and expect a constant Internet connection, wherever they go. Two-thirds of adults (64%) say the Internet is an essential part of their life. One in five adults (19%) say they spend more than 40 hours a week online, an increase from 5% just over ten years ago. For the first time this year, women spend more time online than men.

Over the last decade, better access to the Internet has transformed how we interact with each other. Two-fifths of people (41%) say being online enables them to work more flexibly, and three-quarters (74%) say it keeps them close

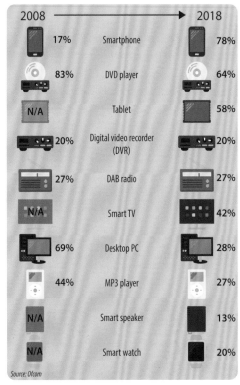

2008 →		2018
17%	Smartphone	78%
83%	DVD player	64%
N/A	Tablet	58%
20%	Digital video recorder (DVR)	20%
27%	DAB radio	27%
N/A	Smart TV	42%
69%	Desktop PC	28%
44%	MP3 player	27%
N/A	Smart speaker	13%
N/A	Smart watch	20%

Source: Ofcom

to friends and family.

The amount of time we spend making phone calls from our mobiles has fallen for the first time, as we increasingly use Internet-based services such as WhatsApp and Facebook Messenger. Using a mobile for phone calls is only considered important by 75% of smartphone users, compared to 92% who consider web browsing to be important.

However, for many people, being online has negative effects. 15 per cent of people say it makes them feel they are always at work, and more than half (54%) admit that connected devices interrupt face-to-face conversations with friends and family. More than two in five (43%) also admit to spending too much time online.

How do you feel without the Internet?

Around a third of people say they feel either cut off (34%) or lost (29%) without the Internet, if they can't get online, and 17% say they find it stressful. Half of all adults (50%) say their life would be boring if they could not access the Internet.

On the other hand, some see a lack of Internet access in a positive light. One in ten feel more productive offline, rising to 15% for 18 to 34–year–olds; and 16% say they feel less distracted.

Smartphone obsession

The proportion of people accessing the Internet on their mobile has increased from 20% almost a decade ago, to 72% in 2018. The average amount of time spent online on a smartphone is two hours 28 minutes a day. This rises to three hours 14 minutes among 18–24s.

How do you feel without the Internet?

'I find it liberating'	'I feel more productive'	'I feel lost without it'	'I feel cut off without it'
10%	10%	29%	10%

Source: Ofcom

72 per cent of adults say their smartphone is their most important device for accessing the internet, 71% say they never turn off their phone, and 78% say they could not live without it.

Ian Macrae, Ofcom's Director of Market Intelligence, said: 'Over the last decade, people's lives have been transformed by the rise of the smartphone, together with better access to the Internet and new services.

'Whether it's working flexibly, keeping up with current affairs or shopping online, we can do more on the move than ever before. But while people appreciate their smartphone as their constant companion, some are finding themselves feeling overloaded when online, or frustrated when they're not.'

Place of phones in society

Older and younger generations disagree on what they see as acceptable smartphone use around others, although many people admit that the way they behave in public on their smartphones is unacceptable in principle.

Three-quarters of people (76%) find it annoying when someone is listening to music, watching videos or playing games loudly on public transport; while 81% object to people using their phone during meal times.

The majority (53%) of adults say they are usually on their phone while watching TV with others. Six in ten people (62%) over 55 think this is unacceptable, but this drops to just two in ten (21%) among those aged 18–34.

Connected commuters

Many commuters now find it essential to be online during their journey, so they can complete tasks in their personal (42%) or professional life (35%). Young adults are more likely to multi–task on their commute: 9% of 18–34s carry out 11 or more online activities, compared to just 1% of over-35s.

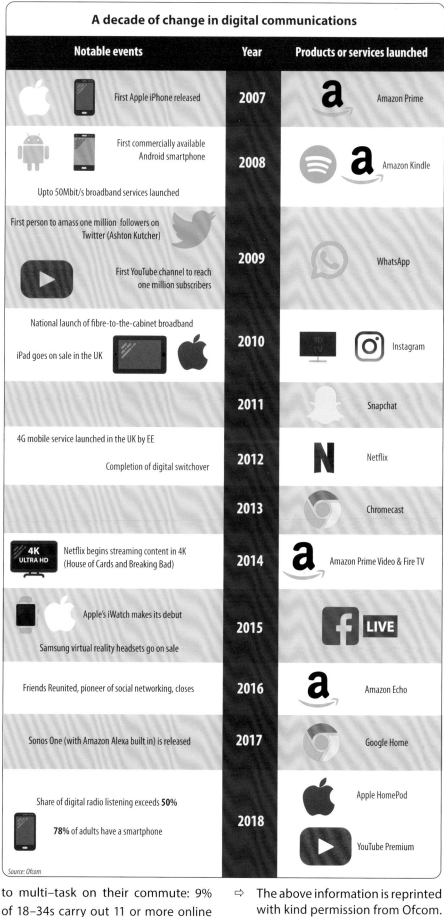

A decade of change in digital communications

Notable events	Year	Products or services launched
First Apple iPhone released	2007	Amazon Prime
First commercially available Android smartphone / Upto 50Mbit/s broadband services launched	2008	Spotify / Amazon Kindle
First person to amass one million followers on Twitter (Ashton Kutcher) / First YouTube channel to reach one million subscribers	2009	WhatsApp
National launch of fibre-to-the-cabinet broadband / iPad goes on sale in the UK	2010	Instagram
	2011	Snapchat
4G mobile service launched in the UK by EE / Completion of digital switchover	2012	Netflix
	2013	Chromecast
Netflix begins streaming content in 4K (House of Cards and Breaking Bad)	2014	Amazon Prime Video & Fire TV
Apple's iWatch makes its debut / Samsung virtual reality headsets go on sale	2015	f LIVE
Friends Reunited, pioneer of social networking, closes	2016	Amazon Echo
Sonos One (with Amazon Alexa built in) is released	2017	Google Home
Share of digital radio listening exceeds **50%** / **78%** of adults have a smartphone	2018	Apple HomePod / YouTube Premium

Source: Ofcom

⇨ The above information is reprinted with kind permission from Ofcom. Please visit www.ofcom.org.uk for further information.

2 August 2018

© 2018 Ofcom

The average person has seven social media accounts

By Colm Hebblethwaite

It can be easy to lose track of how many social media accounts you have. After all, how many people of a certain age never officially closed down their MySpace account?

According to a new report from GlobalWebIndex, the average person now has 7.6 active social media accounts, with 98% of people having at least one social network account. The tech company polled 89,029 people aged 16–64 across 40 countries.

The average number of social networks rises with young consumers to 8.7 for those aged 16–34, although those aged 55–64 still have an average of 4.6 active social accounts.

This multi–networking is seemingly driven by two primary factors. Firstly, the widening of choice of platforms and secondly, the growing degree of specialisation among different networks. So, for example, people turn to Instagram to upload pictures and LinkedIn to network with their business peers.

The trend could be moving downwards however.

The main factor behind this is the emergence of a new entity: that of the mobile-only Internet user. With the shift towards using smartphones to access the Internet more than laptops and tablets, some users do not own any other device aside from their phone.

These users are currently a major proportion of Internet users in the Middle East and Africa. Mobile-only users tend to have significantly less active social media accounts than their multi-device peers, with an average of 5.7.

According to GlobalWebIndex, mobile-only users tend to focus on Facebook and WhatsApp.

Time consuming

The amount of time that people spend on social networks continues to be significant. According to the survey results, the average amount of time spent on social media each day is two hours and 15 minutes.

Facebook continues to dominate the social landscape, with 90% of those surveyed using at least one of its four main services. Facebook Messenger and WhatsApp are used by over 50% of Internet users. In terms of sheer visitor numbers however, YouTube remains the undisputed king.

While news and entertainment are among the main reasons people use social media, it is playing a role in purchase journeys. Over half of the consumers polled said that they are currently following at least one brand and that social networks are the primary channel they use for researching products.

However, this research and interest in a brand's social presence doesn't necessarily translate into purchases. Only 13% of 16–24-year-olds said that a 'buy' button would encourage them to purchase an item over social media.

17 November 2017

⇨ The above information is reprinted with kind permission from Marketing Tech News. Please visit www.marketingtechnews.net for further information.

So long social media: the kids are opting out of the online public square

***An article from* The Conversation.**

THE CONVERSATION

By Felicity Duncan, Assistant Professor of Digital Communication and Social Media, Cabrini College

When my digital media students are sitting, waiting for class to start and staring at their phones, they are not checking Facebook. They're not checking Instagram or Pinterest or Twitter. No, they're catching up on the news of the day by checking out their friends' Stories on Snapchat, chatting in Facebook Messenger or checking in with their friends in a group text. If the time drags, they might switch to Instagram to see what the brands they love are posting, or check in with Twitter for a laugh at some celebrity tweets. But, they tell me, most of the time they eschew the public square of social media for more intimate options.

The times, they are a-changing

For a few years now, alarms have been sounded in various quarters about Facebook's teen problem. In 2013, one author explored why teens are tiring of Facebook, and according to *Time*, more than 11 million young people have fled Facebook since 2011. But many of these articles theorized that teens were moving instead to Instagram (a Facebook-owned property) and other social media platforms. In other words, teen flight was a Facebook problem, not a social media problem.

Today, however, the newest data increasingly support the idea that young people are actually transitioning out of using what we might term broadcast social media – like Facebook and Twitter – and switching instead to using narrowcast tools – like Messenger or Snapchat. Instead of posting generic and sanitized updates for all to see, they are sharing their transient goofy selfies and blow-by-blow descriptions of class with only their closest friends.

For example, in a study published in August last year, the Pew Research Center reported that 49 per cent of smartphone owners between 18 and 29 use messaging apps like Kik, Whatsapp or iMessage, and 41 per cent use apps that automatically delete sent messages, like Snapchat.

For context, note that according to another Pew study, only 37 per cent of people in that age range use Pinterest, only 22 per cent use LinkedIn and only 32 per cent use Twitter. Messaging clearly trumps these more publicly accessible forms of social media.

Admittedly, 82 per cent of people aged 18 to 29 said that they do use Facebook. However, that 82 per cent affirmatively answered the question, 'Do you *ever* use the Internet or a mobile app to use Facebook?' (emphasis added). Having a Facebook account and actually *using* Facebook are two different

Mobile messaging apps particularly popular among young adults

Among smartphone owners the % who use messaging apps
and apps that automatically delete sent messages

	Messaging apps	Auto-delete apps
Total	*36%*	*17%*
Men	37	17
Women	36	18
White, Non-Hispanic	34	18
Black, Non-Hispanic	N/A*	N/A*
Hispanic	N/A*	N/A*
18–29	49	41
30–t49	37	11
50 +	24	4
High school grad or less	30	19
Some college	34	20
College +	45	13
Less than $50,000/yr	37	18
$50,000 +	36	17
Urban	42	22
Suburban	37	15
Rural (n=99 smartphone owners)	22	13

* Because some questions were given to half the respondents, there are not enough cases to allow sufficient statistical analysis for these groups

Source: Pew Research Center. March 17 – April 12, 2015

things. While Pew does have data on how frequently people report using Facebook (70 per cent said at least once a day), those data are not broken down by age. And anecdotal evidence such as what I've gathered from class discussions and assignments suggests that many younger people are logging in to Facebook simply to see what others are posting, rather than creating content of their own. Their photos, updates, likes and dislikes are increasingly shared only in closed gardens like group chat and Snapchat.

Why would they leave?

Although there is not a great deal of published research on the phenomenon, there seem to be several reasons why younger people are opting for messaging over social media. Based on my discussions with around 80 American college students, there appear to be three reasons for choosing something like Snapchat over Facebook.

1. **My gran likes my profile picture**
   As Facebook has wormed its way into our lives, its demographics have shifted dramatically According to Pew, 48 per cent of

Internet users over the age of 65 use Facebook. As social media usage has spread beyond the young, social media have become less attractive to young people. Few college students want their parents to see their Friday night photos.

2. **Permanence and ephemerality**
   Many of the students I've spoken with avoid posting on sites like Facebook because, to quote one student, 'Those pics are there forever!' Having grown up with these platforms, college students are well aware that nothing posted on Facebook is ever truly forgotten, and they are increasingly wary of the implications. Teens engage in complex management of their self-presentation in online spaces; for many college students, platforms like Snapchat, that promise ephemerality, are a welcome break from the need to police their online image.

3. **The professional and the personal** Increasingly, young people are being warned that future employers, college admissions departments and even banks will use their social media

profiles to form assessments. In response, many of them seem to be using social media more strategically. For example, a number of my students create multiple profiles on sites like Twitter, under various names. They carefully curate the content they post on their public profiles on Facebook or LinkedIn, and save their real, private selves for other platforms.

Is this a problem?

We may be seeing the next evolution in digital media. Just as young people were the first to migrate on to platforms like Facebook and Twitter, they may now be the first to leave and move on to something new.

This exodus of young people from publicly accessible social media to messaging that is restricted to smaller groups has a number of implications, both for the big businesses behind social media and for the public sphere more generally.

From a corporate perspective, the shift is potentially troubling. If young people are becoming less likely

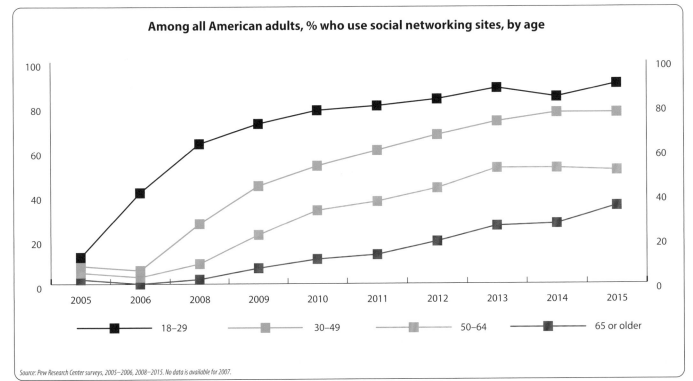

Among all American adults, % who use social networking sites, by age

18–29   30–49   50–64   65 or older

Source: Pew Research Center surveys, 2005–2006, 2008–2015. No data is available for 2007.

to provide personal details about themselves to online sites, the digital advertising machine that runs on such data (described in detail by Joe Turow in his book *The Daily You*) may face some major headwinds.

For example, if young people are no longer 'liking' things on Facebook, the platform's long-term value to advertisers may erode. Currently, Facebook uses data it gathers about users' 'likes' and 'shares' to target advertising at particular individuals. So, hypothetically, if you 'like' an animal rescue, you may see advertisements for PetSmart on Facebook. This type of precision targeting has made Facebook into a formidable advertising platform; in 2015, the company earned almost US$18 billion, virtually all of it from advertising. If young people stop feeding the Facebook algorithm by clicking 'like', this revenue could be in jeopardy.

From the perspective of parents and older social media users, this shift can also seem troubling. Parents who may be accustomed to monitoring at least some proportion of their children's online lives may find themselves increasingly shut out. On the other hand, for the growing number of adults who use these platforms to stay in touch with their own peer networks, exchange news and information, and network, this change may go virtually unnoticed. And, indeed, for the many older people who have never understood the attraction of airing one's laundry on social media, the shift may even seem like a positive maturation among younger users.

From a social or academic perspective, the shift is both encouraging, in that it is supportive of calls for more reticence online, and also troubling.

As more and more political activity migrates online, and social media play a role in a number of important social movement activities, the exodus of the young could mean that they become less exposed to important social justice issues and political ideas. If college students spend most of their media time on group text and Snapchat, there is less opportunity for new ideas to enter their social networks. Emerging research is documenting the ways in which our use of social media for news monitoring can lead us to consume only narrow, partisan news. If young people opt to use open messaging services even less, they may further reduce their exposure to news and ideas that challenge their current beliefs.

The great promise of social media was that they would create a powerful and open public sphere, in which ideas could spread and networks of political action could form. If it is true that the young are turning aside from these platforms, and spending most of their time with messaging apps that connect only those who are already connected, the political promise of social media may never be realised.

2 February 2016

⇨ The above information is reprinted with kind permission from *The Conversation*. Please visit www. theconversation.com for further information.

Why did you use social media today?

Social cyberpsychology researcher Dr Lisa Orchard takes a look at our motivations for posting on social media.

Imagine the scenario – you are meeting a work colleague for breakfast in your local coffee shop. You are halfway through a conversation when the waiter brings over your coffees and croissants. Your friend nods along as you continue to chat.

However, you notice that your friend is casually rearranging the table décor and, once the conversation has a natural pause, takes the opportunity to capture the moment with an artistic photo to be uploaded to Instagram.

Within a heartbeat, the update has been made, the phone is placed back on the table, and the conversation picks up where it left off. After the meeting, you say your goodbyes, and catch a bus.

You take a seat, get out your phone, and spend the entire journey scrolling through your social media channels. Later that evening you sit down to watch *Love Island*, and again take out your phone. You send a Facebook message to your friend – 'it's about to start'. Three dots later, you receive a series of heart emojis.

Social media runs in the background of our lives; a shared communication stream ready to be tapped into whenever needed. But what motivates us to pick up our phone, and click that app logo?

The mainstream media may have us believe that social media usage is out of our control. However, we could take a more positive view. Uses and gratifications theory suggests that we are active in our use.

It is argued that users selectively choose media in order to fulfil specific motivations. A few years ago, we created the Social Media Motivations Scale (SMMS) in order to tease out some of these motivations.

Although not an exhaustive list, our research identified ten possible motivations that may drive our use: procrastination, freedom of expression, conformity, information exchange,

making new connections, ritualistic, social maintenance, escapism, recreation, and experimentation.

It is important to note that we may have many motivations for using social media, and these will change throughout the day.

Think back to the scenario – each occurrence of social media reflects a different reason: uploading a photo at the coffee shop may reflect ritualistic use or perhaps free expression; the bus ride is a by-product of procrastination; and the private communication stream stems from social maintenance.

We also found that different people were drawn to different motivations. Our individual differences (that is our personality, age and sex) were found to predict the motivations we held.

For instance, older users were motivated by conformity more so than younger users. On the other hand, younger users were more motivated by procrastination and finding new connections. Females use social media in an attempt to maintain their existing social network, whilst males

scored higher on the motivation of experimentation (i.e. pretending to be someone else).

Personality findings were also found throughout. For instance, those high in neuroticism (anxiety) were more motivated by escapism than lower scorers; whilst extroverts were more motivated by recreation and new connections than introverts.

The next step is to see how this all feeds in to actual social media usage. Dr Chris Fullwood and I have collected some more data using the SMMS, and we plan to explore the relationship of the scale with Facebook behavioural scales to explore how motivations feed into in-app feature use and our social dependency with Facebook.

17 July 2018

⇨ The above information is reprinted with kind permission from University of Wolverhampton. Please visit www.wlv.ac.uk for further information.

Young people spend a third of their leisure time on devices

Is technology making us less sociable? A look at how technology has influenced our leisure time.

Young people spent more than a third of their overall leisure time – around 14 hours per week – using a device in 2015, new analysis shows.

Men aged 25 and under use devices such as mobile phones, tablets, e-readers and laptops the most. Device use occupied 35% of their leisure time, whereas for women it was 29%.

The highest share of time devoted to device use was when people were pursuing hobbies, computing or playing games, which is to be expected, as computing naturally requires device use. Resting had the second highest share of device use, which can include searching the web and chatting using a mobile phone.

People in this age group are more likely to be heavier users of social media. This may explain their high use of devices compared with other age groups.

People are spending less leisure time being active

Compared to 2000, people in 2015 spent less of their leisure time, on average, on activities like sports and cultural pursuits. The 2015 survey included the category 'device use' which could contribute to the difference in other leisure pursuits.

Adults aged 19 to 64 are advised by the NHS to undertake a mixture of aerobic and strength exercises every week. This could include 150 minutes of aerobic activity and two days per week spent doing exercises that use all muscle groups.

In 2015 to 2016, 26% of adults in England were classified as inactive (carrying out less than 30 minutes of physical activity per week). According to the NHS, people in the UK are around 20% less active now than they were in the 1960s.

The NHS says this is down to varying factors like the rise of car ownership, and more recently, the popularity of sedentary activities such as playing video games and computing.

People aged 56 and over performed the smallest proportion of active leisure; however, this includes elderly people who are recommended to do fewer hours.

In terms of how these numbers have changed, people aged 46 to 55 years took a lower share of active leisure time compared to those of a similar age in 2000, the biggest decrease in any age category.

Are we becoming less sociable?

In 2015, people spent an average of around six hours per week socialising – a fall of 12.7% since 2000. When compared with total leisure time available – 38 hours per week for women and 43 hours per week for men – this is a small amount of the total.

Comparatively, mass media consumption, for example reading, listening to music or watching television, accounts for around half of all leisure time taken. People may be using mobile phones to socialise when they're watching television, but it's not necessarily face-to-face communication.

It's possible that with increased device use, people are becoming less likely to go out of their way to meet up and socialise. Easy internet access enables people to talk to friends via social media apps, but they're still doing so alone.

The data show that, of all leisure time spent using a device, 46% of this time is spent alone compared with 29% without a device.

19 December 2017

⇨ The above information is reprinted with kind permission from the Office for National Statistics. Please visit www.ons.gov.uk for further information.

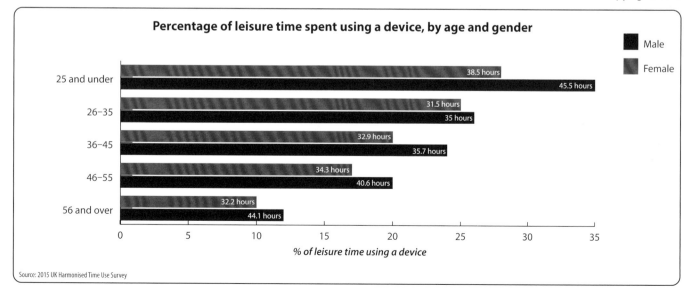

Percentage of leisure time spent using a device, by age and gender

■ Male
▨ Female

25 and under	Female 38.5 hours	Male 45.5 hours
26–35	Female 31.5 hours	Male 35 hours
36–45	Female 32.9 hours	Male 35.7 hours
46–55	Female 34.3 hours	Male 40.6 hours
56 and over	Female 32.2 hours	Male 44.1 hours

% of leisure time using a device

Source: 2015 UK Harmonised Time Use Survey

Teenagers shun homework for social media and video games

Teenagers are far more likely to spend their time on social media and gaming after school than they are to be doing homework, according to a new UCL-led study.

Around 3,500 UK teenagers, whose lives have been closely followed from birth by the *Millennium Cohort Study*, were asked to keep a detailed time use diary for one weekday and one weekend day. The data, which the teens recorded either via a smartphone app or online, has shed new light on how young people spend their time.

Around half of the teens surveyed reported spending some time on social media on a weekday. This proportion was considerably higher for girls at six in ten (61%), compared to 39% among boys. One in ten teenagers who reported being on social media had spent upwards of three hours a day online, though the average time spent was one hour 21 minutes per day.

For boys, gaming was an even more popular pastime than social media; almost half (48%) of all boys had spent time on video games, and of these,

12% reported spending in excess of five hours a day gaming. Just one in ten girls had notched up any time at all on video games.

By comparison, the teenagers' diaries revealed that just 40% did homework on an average weekday, and that boys were significantly less likely to than their female peers – 35 per cent of boys compared to 44 per cent of girls. Those who did do homework, spent an average of one hour 13 minutes doing it.

The researchers at Centre for Longitudinal Studies (CLS), based at the UCL Institute of Education, found some other striking gender differences. Teenage girls spent about 27 minutes more time on average on a weekday getting ready (a total of one hour 12 minutes on average) compared to their male peers. Girls were also much more likely to help out around the house, with 31 per cent reporting doing chores at home on a weekday, compared to just 19 per cent of their male peers. And while, overall, very few teenagers spent any time reading

in their spare time (just one in ten), this was significantly more popular as a pastime for girls.

But when it came to sports and other physical activity outside of school, these were more common among boys; 46 per cent of teenage boys had recorded these in their weekday diaries, compared to 39 per cent of girls.

However, sedentary forms of entertainment, including watching TV, playing video games and listening to music, were collectively far more popular than sport for both genders. 72 per cent of all teens spent on average just over two-and-a-half hours per day on these sedentary types of activities. These figures may be of some concern, particularly when considered alongside the high levels of obesity among this age group.

Professor Emla Fitzsimons (UCL Institute of Education), Principal Investigator of the *Millennium Cohort Study*, said: 'These findings provide unparalleled insight into how young people in the UK spend their time. Not only that, but combined with other information we have collected from this group through our surveys, there is now enormous potential to better understand how different aspects of teenagers' lives fit together.

'For example, is there a relationship between girls' use of social media and their mental health? Does the popularity of social media and gaming play any part in the obesity crisis among young people? These are really important questions, and this rich new data will be instrumental in answering them.'

11 May 2018

⇨ The above information is reprinted with kind permission from University College London. Please visit www.ucl.ac.uk for further information.

My generation's dark addiction to social media

Why do we have such a desire to showcase our daily lives on social media? Why do we feel the need to constantly prove that we are living happy and fulfilled lives?

By Shannon Rawlins

I often sit on the train and watch the person in front of me as they flick through their mobile phone. What I see concerns me. Often, they just refresh their Instagram or Facebook feed, over and over again, lingering every so often on someone's new profile picture or upload of the photos from 'last night'. What do they feel when they stare at these photos of other people's lives? Jealousy? Insecurity? A sense of inadequacy? Probably all of the above. So why then, do millennials spend an average of over two hours per day using social media apps such as Snapchat, Instagram and Facebook?

You are probably expecting the writer of this article to be some middle-aged old fart, bemoaning the 'state of the young generation'. But no. I am 18 years old. I am a millennial too. I had Snapchat, I had Instagram, I had all the works. But I became disillusioned. And to be honest, it surprises me that the vast majority of my peers are so *blind* to the extent and toxicity of our insidious addiction to social media.

Blind to the absurdity of this mystifying need we possess to constantly check up on our peers' lives. Blind to our seeming incapacity to enjoy a night out without taking countless photos to post the next day. Blind to the fact that girls choose what to wear based on what will look best through an iPhone camera lens.

I am worried for the future of my own generation. We seem more concerned with the persona we have cultivated online rather than with who we really are. Why? Why do we live such a lie? On a night out, all I see are teenage girls desperate to capture the moment to post on their Snapchat story. 'Hey look', they seem to say. 'I'm drinking, I'm having fun. I have a life. Do you?'

This poisonous addiction is twofold. Not only do we have an incessant need to track other people's social media accounts but also to constantly update our own. It is something of a vicious cycle, leading inevitably to a generation of insecure, insular and cagey individuals.

So I ask again: why do we spend so much of our lives on social media?

Certainly to some extent, we can attribute it to egoism; we want to make sure as many people as possible are aware of just how wonderful our lives are. But on a deeper level, is there also that intrinsic, primitive desire to *compete*?

So-and-so posts a photo of their holiday in Portugal, suntanned, laughing, drinking a cocktail. Joe Bloggs stuck in dreary London feels a twinge of jealousy. Said Joe Bloggs hits the like button but makes sure he captures his night at the pub for his Snapchat story, just to make sure so-and-so in Portugal knows he's enjoying his life too. Joe Bloggs probably doesn't really feel any better about himself.

It is an utterly paradoxical addiction; scrolling through social media causes us to feel bitter and insecure – this should be enough to makes us want to delete all of our accounts, to be free of the burden of our addiction. Yet somehow, it's not.

I suppose most probably just try and pretend that the niggly twinge of jealousy and discomfort, as they scroll through their newsfeed or flick through Snapchat, isn't really there. All I did was choose not to ignore it; I am by no means immune to the impact of social media. I simply realised that it was making me feel depressed, anxious and insecure, and chose to do something about it.

It has been proven that social media –on the whole – has a negative impact on our mental health and happiness levels. Participants in numerous psychological studies about social media have tended to experience a sharp decline in their moods after scrolling through mindless videos and pictures or snapshots of their friends and family.

Social media does not bring people together; it drives us apart. People become locked inside their own self-constructed virtual world, and develop a heightened sensitivity to how they – and their social media profiles – are perceived by others.

I believe that social media is utterly toxic. It is altering the way we live our lives, how we form relations and connect with our peers. We seem to value the virtual world more than the real one.

So be honest with yourself. Ask yourself this simple question: is social media really making you any happier?

20 July 2018

⇨ The above information is reprinted with kind permission from Shout Out UK. Please visit www.shoutoutuk.org for further information.

Facebook to launch 'take a break' pop-up warnings to help children spend less time on social media

By Charles Hymas

Facebook has attempted to counter a growing public and political backlash by introducing 'digital wellbeing' tools that enable users to spend less time on its apps.

Users of Facebook and Instagram will be able to create pop-up alerts to limit their time on the apps, block push notifications for fixed periods and get updates on the time they have spent on the social networks each day.

The changes, announced on Wednesday and to be introduced around the world over coming weeks, come amid growing concern at the potential damage excessive use of social media is having on the mental and emotional health of children.

Campaigners, however, said the moves did not address online harms like bullying or inappropriate content and failed to provide a default mode that would require people to opt out of time limits or blocking notifications.

LSE professor Sonia Livingstone, a board member of the UK Council for Child Internet Safety, said default time limits would be a 'great next step' while regulation was still needed to make the firms more accountable and transparent about how they protected children from harms.

'We still need regulation,' she said. 'Facebook might decide in a year's time it is too expensive and what is going to make Snapchat and the long tail of other companies do it? It's great that Facebook innovates but it's insufficient across the industry.'

The Telegraph has launched a campaign for a statutory duty of care on social media and gaming firms to protect children from online harms.

Ameet Ranadive, Instagram's product director of wellbeing, said it was a 'first step' to address concerns: 'Our long term goal with all of these tools is to give people more insights and control into how they can manage their time and experience on Facebook and Instagram.'

Each of the three tools are accessed on smartphones and tablets, but not desktops, by clicking through to a dashboard showing the average daily time for each of the apps on that device.

The feature displays a daily average over the past seven days, and each of those seven days' usage. It is based on the time the app is open rather than actual activity. However, it does not show the time spent on Facebook across different devices, for example, if users access Facebook on both a phone and tablet.

Another tool, called 'Set Daily Reminder' allows the user to set up an alert for the amount of time in five-minute increments they want to spend online. A notification will then pop up after hitting the time limit.

A separate 'Notification Settings' tool allows the user to mute push notifications for between 15 minutes and eight hours. The notifications can then be picked up once the 'mute' period is over.

Asked if it accepted the need for parental control over children's time online, Facebook said not, but added: 'Our hope is that these tools foster conversations between parents and teens about the online habits that are right for them.'

It also ruled out for the time being a default setting so people had to opt out of a time limit or muted notifications, an alert that would automatically shut down the app or recommending a 'healthy' length of time online based on its research.

'As we learn about how people use the tools and get feedback from our community, we'll continue to refine the alerts and settings,' said a

spokesman. It said it would also review how it directed users to the tools.

While welcomed as a first step, campaigners said more was needed. Baroness Kidron, the film producer and children's rights campaigner, said: 'I am glad they're finally thinking about better design but this is not enough. They have to do 'default high' so they take responsibility for their design and don't consistently push the onus onto the children themselves.'

The Royal Society for Public Health said Facebook was moving in the right direction but added: 'We would like to see settings that help people manage their use and promote positive mental health and well-being enabled by default and prominently signposted, rather than leaving the responsibility with users to opt-in to changes that may be buried and hard to access, or that need to be repeatedly reactivated.'

Laura Randall, NSPCC Associate Head of Child Safety Online said: 'Time limits do not address the fact that there are still no consistent child safety standards in place. Apps, sites and games continue to allow violent and sexual content to be accessed by children; and sexual predators are free to roam their platforms targeting and grooming young people.

'This lack of responsibility is why the legislation the Government has committed to, must include a mandatory child safety code with an independent regulator to enforce consequences for those who don't follow those rules.'

The move follows a similar initiative by Apple which offers iPhone and iPad users a 'Screen Time' dashboard highlighting how much time they have spent on which apps, how many notifications they receive, how often they pick up their device and how their usage patterns compare to the average.

In January, Facebook founder Mark Zuckerberg announced changes to prioritise posts from friends and family over public content as part of an attempt to counter criticism that it was turning people into passive consumers rather than encouraging active 'meaningful' contacts.

1 August 2018

'Fear of missing out' driving social media addiction, study suggests

Fear of missing out, or 'FOMO', is among the biggest causes of social media addiction, a new study suggests.

Psychologists at Nottingham Trent University investigated the factors driving addiction to social networking sites among people in the UK.

The study investigated a range of factors relating to participants' personalities and their social media use.

Writing in the international journal *CyberPsychology, Behavior and Social Networking*, the team found that about 5% of participants could be classed as being at high risk of addiction.

When looking at the collective factors driving their addictive behaviour, FOMO, irrational beliefs and poor mental health explained participants' social media addiction almost entirely.

And when they looked at each of the factors individually, the researchers found that FOMO was the most significant contributing factor to explain the emergence of social media addiction.

FOMO relates to a feeling that friends and connections are leading more interesting and rewarding lives, creating a desire to stay continually connected with what others are doing online.

Facebook, Twitter, Snapchat, Instagram, LinkedIn, YouTube and Tumblr were all used by participants, with Facebook being the most widely used (99% of participants) followed by Instagram (72%).

The majority of participants used four different social networking sites.

Almost a third of participants (32%) claimed to use social networking sites 'a great deal' every day – the most amount of time – with the same figure claiming to have suffered problems due to their social networking use.

The study also found that those at high risk of addiction used significantly more social media platforms.

'When experiencing FOMO chronically, it could lead to addictive behaviour towards social media use,' said Dr Halley Pontes, a psychologist in Nottingham Trent University's School of Social Sciences.

He said: 'It is important to know that FOMO may be worsened by the fact that we are being constantly reminded about what we are missing out on via all the notifications we receive to our phones. One potential strategy to curb FOMO may be to manage which notifications we want to receive.'

'Although the origin of FOMO may vary from one person to another, it is often a result of a deficit in psychological need, such as social connection. For this reason, living a socially fulfilling life where psychological needs toward social connections can be met may also help overcome anxiety associated with FOMO.'

'Previous studies have tended to focus exclusively on Facebook addiction, but we have gone beyond this to examine a range of social networking sites. We hope the findings might also be of use to therapists in helping them to refine their treatment.'

Earlier this year, research by Dr Pontes revealed that addiction to video games was affecting people psychologically and physically, as well as having a negative impact on personal and social relationships.

The latest study also involved the Cairnmiller Institute in Australia and the University of Athens.

4 June 2018

Social media is as harmful as alcohol and drugs for millennials

*An article by **The Conversation**.*

THE CONVERSATION

Tony Rao, Visiting Lecturer in Old Age Psychiatry, King's College London

The word 'addiction' brings to mind alcohol and drugs. Yet, over the past 20 years, a new type of addiction has emerged: addiction to social media. It may not cause physical harms, such as those caused by tobacco and alcohol, but it has the potential to cause long-term damage to our emotions, behaviour and relationships.

While the older generation – those born in the baby boom period shortly after World War II – had alcohol and drugs as their vice, the younger generation – the so-called millennials – have social media as theirs. The millennials, born between 1984 and 2005, have embraced the digital age, using technology to relax and interact with others. Social media is a big deal for them; it is a lifeline to the outside world.

Although people of all ages use social media, it is more harmful for younger users than it is for older people.

All consuming

Addiction may seem a bit of a strong word to use in the context of social media, but addiction refers to any behaviour that is pleasurable and is the only reason to get through the day. Everything else pales into insignificance. Millennials may not get liver damage or lung cancer from social media, but it can be damaging nonetheless.

The harm lies in their change in behaviour. Their addiction means spending increasing amount of time online to produce the same pleasurable effect, and it means social media is the main activity they engage in above all others. It also means taking away attention from other tasks, experiencing unpleasant feelings from reducing or stopping interaction with social media and restarting the activity very soon after stopping completely.

We should also be concerned about the effect of social media on sleep and doing less 'offline', such as making time for work responsibilities and direct face-to-face social interaction. It has also been linked to depression and loneliness, both of which may be the cause or the effect of social media addiction.

Millennials report compulsively checking social network profiles and updates. They can make riskier decisions and be open to online exploitation. They often mistakenly believe that, if things go wrong, they will get help from their online community, even if this community consists of relative strangers.

Lacking self-reflection

Most of us rely partly on the ability to reflect on our thinking, feeling and behaving to form our own self-image. The problem with social media is that self-image relies mainly on others and their opinions. A recent study found higher narcissism (an exaggerated self-image of intelligence, academic reputation or attractiveness) in millennial college students, compared with previous generations. This does not bode well for a society where self-reflection is key to making informed and balanced decisions.

The digital age has changed the nature of addictions in millennials, who have replaced one maladaptive behaviour with another. Social media certainly looks as if it has replaced alcohol as a way of social interaction with others. It is perhaps no surprise that, over the past ten years, there has been a 20% rise in the proportion of 16- to 24-year-olds who are teetotal. Ten years ago it was 17%. It is now 24%. Spending time online now seems more desirable than spending time in a pub with friends.

There is no recognised treatment for social media addiction. Although we are starting to become aware of the problem, there is no classification of social media addiction as a mental disorder in the same way as substance misuse. If we want this to happen, there needs to be a clearer definition of the symptoms and progression over time. We will need to answer some key questions, such as: does it run in families? Are there blood tests that can distinguish it from other mental disorders? And will it respond to drugs or psychological therapies? We still have more questions than answers.

12 June 2018

Teenagers are getting plastic surgery to look like their snapchat selfies

Patients want to look the way photo-editing apps make them look.

By Chelsea Ritschell

Teenagers are undergoing plastic surgery to look like they do in their filtered selfies – and it may be a sign they are suffering from an underlying mental health condition.

In addition to unicorn horns and dog ears, Snapchat and Instagram also offer perfecting filters that smooth skin, thin your face and change your eye colour – photo-editing technology that has resulted in a new mental illness scientists are calling 'Snapchat dysmorphia.'

'A new phenomenon called Snapchat dysmorphia has popped up, where patients are seeking out surgery to help them appear like the filtered versions of themselves,' said Dr Neelam Vashi, director of the Boston University Cosmetic and Laser Centre.

These are the terrifying plastic surgery apps aimed at young girls

The study, published in *JAMA Facial Plastic Surgery Viewpoint,* found apps like Snapchat and photo-editing Facetune are to blame – as they allow selfies to achieve a level of physical 'perfection' previously seen only in celebrity or beauty magazines.

According to plastic surgeons and researchers, patients are no longer bringing in photos of celebrities, they are bringing in pictures of their selfies – edited to look like perfect versions of themselves.

Dr Vashi said: 'A little adjusting on Facetune can smoothen out skin, and make teeth look whiter and eyes and lips bigger. A quick share on Instagram and the likes and comments start rolling in.'

Now millennials are trying to replicate the perfection in real life by seeking out treatments that contour cheekbones, straighten or reduce nose size, or make a person look slimmer.

As these images become the norm on social media, and in real life, the idea of what is attractive worldwide also changes – which can affect self-esteem and trigger body dysmorphic disorder (BDD) or Snapchat dysmorphia, a term coined by Dr Tijion Esho, a cosmetic doctor.

BDD is an excessive preoccupation with a perceived flaw in appearance often characterised by people going to great – and at times unhealthy – lengths to hide their imperfections.

The mental illness, classified on the obsessive-compulsive spectrum, is surprisingly common, affecting one in every 50 people – and growing, as millennials are influenced by what they see online.

Dr Esho, who will turn away patients who seem overly obsessed with resembling filters, previously said: 'We now see photos of ourselves daily via the social platforms we use, which arguably makes us more critical of ourselves. Patients using pictures of celebrities or Snapchat–filtered versions of themselves as reference points is OK.

'The danger is when this is not just a reference point, but it becomes how the patient sees themselves, or the patient wants to look exactly like that image.'

And these filtered selfies can be even more dangerous for people with BDD.

Dr Vashi said: 'Filtered selfies especially can have harmful effects on adolescents or those with BDD because these groups may more severely internalise this beauty.'

One survey of plastic surgeons found 55 per cent last year reported seeing patients who wanted to improve their appearance in selfies – in comparison to the 13 per cent the American Academy of Facial Plastic and Reconstructive Surgeons reported seeing in 2013.

This is coupled with the reported increase in plastic surgery patients younger than 30.

Rather than going under the knife, Dr Vashi recommends that people suffering from BDD seek psychological interventions such as cognitive behavioural therapy – as surgery can worsen underlying BDD.

'Filtered selfies can make people lose touch with reality, creating the expectation we are supposed to look perfectly primped all the time,' said Dr Vashi. 'This can be especially harmful for teens and those with BDD, and it is important for providers to understand the implications of social media on body image to better treat and counsel our patients.'

The emergence of Snapchat dysmorphia comes after previous studies found social media negatively impacts self-esteem and increases the risk of mental health issues.

In a 2015 report from the Office for National Statistics, more than a quarter of teenagers who use social media for more than three hours a day were found to have problems related to mental health.

For patients who do display symptoms of BDD, the researchers and doctors recommend additional screening to check for underlying problems.

'Further questions should be asked to screen for any element of body dysmorphia,' Dr Esho said. 'Treating patients that do show those red flags is not only unethical, but also detrimental to the patient, as they need something that no needle or scalpel can ever provide.'

4 August 2018

Admit it, older people – you are addicted to your phones, too

Over-reliance on mobiles isn't just the scourge of the young, and it has a damaging effect on families.

By Sophia Ankel

My mother likes to sit with her legs crossed on the sofa, glasses balanced on her nose, while she scrolls through her iPhone. I don't know whether she is commenting on a friend's family photo album, crushing candy or liking a meme with the caption: 'Tonight's forecast: 99% chance of wine', but I do know that this is not the first time I catch her like this. My father opts for the 'I'll be with you shortly' line, which he delivers with a very serious look on his face as he aggressively taps away on his phone. I have learned by now that this is my cue to leave him alone for the next 10 minutes. As much as they don't like admitting it, both of my parents are just as addicted to their phones as I am.

Growing up, we are constantly reminded that young people are the demographic most affected by technology. We are the 'antisocial social club', those who prefer to text our friends in the same room rather than having to make eye-contact with them. We are the 'digital natives', ruining the English language because we favour using heart-eye emojis to tell someone we fancy them, instead of spelling it out. We are 'generation mute', unable to bear phone calls because apparently the awkwardness of calling someone up is just too real. And even though I can recognise myself in some of the never-ending studies that reveal to us the extent of our social media addiction, warning us that we are slowly turning into tech-zombies, we should at least consider that it's not only us young 'uns any more.

There's the rise of the Instagram mums, who like to post an abundance of cute baby pictures, showcasing their seemingly (and oddly) put-together lifestyles and sharing their many #momfeelings along the way. Or the surge of over-55-year-olds who are beginning to occupy and curate Facebook. They are the so-called 'Facebook mum generation', a growing group of parents that like to overshare and, in the process, are slowly pushing out young people who can't bear to see another one of mum's embarrassing gin-and-tonic-on-a-holiday selfies. While many millennials are

slowly leaving Facebook because our timeline seems to only clog up with fake news, dog videos and repetitive memes these days, our parents might see the platform as a way of keeping up with the social lives of their old schoolmates or, paradoxically, in my mother's case, 'to see what my children are up to since phone calls have been running a bit dry'. They're a little late to the party, but are still arriving in their droves, with Facebook expecting its largest growth of new members joining the platform in the UK to be among the over-55s users this year (a predicted 500,000, in fact).

And while all of this might be fine, and even a little humorous, new research suggests that parents' technology addiction is negatively affecting their children's behaviour. According to the study, 40% of mothers and 32% of fathers have admitted to having some sort of phone addiction. This has led to a significant fall in verbal interactions within families and even a decline in mothers encouraging their children. 'Technoference' is the term used here to describe the increasing trend that sees people switching their attention away from those around them to check their phones instead – one that seems to be infiltrating far beyond friendship circles and now also into family life. And by family life, I mean not only young teens and children who are glued to their phones or tablets, but also their parents, who are now joining in on the antisocial fun. What are the consequences if we don't deal with this? And why don't we recognise it in the first place, when all the signs are there?

There is no denying that I get annoyed when I receive the 'I'll be with you shortly line' from a parent, when all I want to do is ask one question. But, at the same time, leaving the room to wait until my father is finished with his 'serious business' (i.e. *Farmville*), has now become the norm. Whether you want to escape your pestering children for a bit, or want to stay up late flicking through Twitter, know that wanting to do all of this is normal. We – your children – know how addictive it can be and how difficult it is to switch off. But before calling us out and telling us to 'put our phones away at the table' or even worse, pulling up statistics of how damaging social media can be for us, maybe lead by example and consider how much time you spend on the phone as well as how this is impacting your children and your relationship with them. Maybe in this way we can work on our addiction together.

21 July 2018

⇨ The above information is reprinted with kind permission from *The Guardian.* Please visit www.theguardian.com for further information.

Digital addiction: how technology keeps us hooked

An article from **The Conversation.**

By Raian Ali, Associate Professor in Computing and Informatics, Bournemouth University; Emily Arden-Close, Senior Lecturer in Psychology, Bournemouth University; and John McAlaney, Principal Academic in Psychology, Bournemouth University

The World Health Organization is to include 'gaming disorder', the inability to stop gaming, into the International Classification of Diseases. By doing so, the WHO is recognising the serious and growing problem of digital addiction. The problem has also been acknowledged by Google, which recently announced that it will begin focusing on 'Digital Wellbeing'.

Although there is a growing recognition of the problem, users are still not aware of exactly how digital technology is designed to facilitate addiction. We're part of a research team that focuses on digital addiction and here are some of the techniques and mechanisms that digital media use to keep you hooked.

Compulsive checking

Digital technologies, such as social networks, online shopping and games, use a set of persuasive and motivational techniques to keep users returning. These include 'scarcity' (a snap or status is only temporarily available, encouraging you to get online quickly); 'social proof' (20,000 users retweeted an article so you should go online and read it); 'personalisation' (your news feed is designed to filter and display news based on your interest); and 'reciprocity' (invite more friends to get extra points, and once your friends are part of the network it becomes much more difficult for you or them to leave).

Technology is designed to utilise the basic human need to feel a sense of belonging and connection with others. So, a fear of missing out, commonly known as FOMO, is at the heart of many features of social media design.

Groups and forums in social media promote active participation. Notifications and 'presence features' keep people notified of each others' availability and activities in real-time so that some start to become compulsive checkers. This includes 'two ticks' on instant messaging tools, such as Whatsapp. Users can see whether their message has been delivered and read. This creates pressure on each person to respond quickly to the other.

The concepts of reward and infotainment, material which is both entertaining and informative, are also crucial for 'addictive' designs. In social networks, it is said that 'no news is not good news'. So, their design strives always to provide content and prevent disappointment. The seconds of anticipation for the 'pull to refresh' mechanism on smartphone apps, such as Twitter, is similar to pulling the lever of a slot machine and waiting for the win.

Most of the features mentioned above have roots in our non–tech world. Social networking sites have not created any new or fundamentally different styles of interaction between humans. Instead they have vastly amplified the speed and ease with which these interactions can occur, taking them to a higher speed, and scale.

Addiction and awareness

People using digital media do exhibit symptoms of behavioural addiction. These include salience, conflict and mood modification when they check their online profiles regularly. Often people feel the need to engage with digital devices even if it is inappropriate or dangerous for them to do so. If disconnected or unable to interact as desired, they become preoccupied with missing opportunities to engage with their online social networks.

According to the UK's communications regulator Ofcom, 15 million UK internet users (around 34% of all Internet users) have tried a 'digital detox'. After being offline, 33% of participants reported feeling an increase in productivity, 27% felt a sense of liberation and 25% enjoyed life more. But the report also highlighted that 16% of participants experienced the fear of missing out, 15% felt lost and 14% 'cut-off'. These figures suggest that people want to spend less time online, but they may need help to do so.

At the moment, tools that enable people to be in control of their online experience, presence and online interaction remain very primitive. There seem to be unwritten expectations for users to adhere to social norms of cyberspace once they accept participation.

But unlike other mediums for addiction, such as alcohol, technology can play a role in making its usage more informed and conscious. It is possible to detect whether someone is using a phone or social network in an anxious, uncontrolled manner. Similar to online gambling, users should have available help if they wish. This could be a self-exclusion and lock-out scheme. Users can allow software to alert them when their usage pattern indicates risk.

The borderline between software which is legitimately immersive and software which can be seen as 'exploitation-ware' remains an open question. Transparency of digital persuasion design and education about critical digital literacy could be potential solutions.

12 June 2018

Chapter 2

Safer Internet Day 2018 – a parent's perspective

Trying to keep your family and yourself safe online isn't just a matter of deploying bigger and better technologies and gadgets, says Martin Cooper AMBCS RITTech, BCS' Content Manager.

The Internet is humankind's greatest technological achievement. As a parent, it is also the greatest source of headaches and worry. Striking a balance between keeping kids safe and allowing them the freedom to explore, to learn, to share and to communicate is nightmarish. And it's made even more difficult because the Internet, culture, expectations and software all change at such a frightening rate.

And so, it is very important that BCS lends its support to Safer Internet Day 2018. As a BCS member – and as a parent – I applaud its agenda for a safer and a more respectful Internet.

Lotus eating

A few years ago, I thought I was doing a good job when it came to internet safety. I had configured my home network and broadband carefully and believed it was a solid and reliable playpen for my children. Right up until they showed me I was completely wrong.

We'll look at those technical aids later. They are useful, but not the whole answer.

First though, I would like to share my conclusion. And it is this: keeping your kids safer online is, in my experience, about discussion. Discussing the risks – as you understand them. Discussing how to mitigate those risks and discussing how those mitigations work. And, also, discussing the bad guys' motivations and tactics.

My epiphany came when, being absolutely sure I had rigged up a perfect and impervious digital baby sitter, I found my son and his friend playing Minecraft online with 'some boys in Japan'. This was a few years ago and configuring Minecraft PE – the tablet version – to play online was pretty tricky. They had watched some YouTube videos about how to connect with other gamers across the internet, followed the instructions and were busy 'pwning' each other.

My confidence needed reassessing and my purist's faith in technology took a battering. As a family we started to use discussion to supplement technical countermeasures. My wife did not know about any of this, so discussing it together seemed like a good idea.

Nothing is perfect, of course, but through using some of these ideas – we have survived. Thus far.

Discussion

'If it's too good to be true, it probably isn't.': Download the latest game for free. Free apps. Earn lots of money today. The Internet is groaning with ads that promise something for nothing. In our family we found getting into the habit of discussing and deconstructing these ads to be very useful. What's the seller's angle? How are they making money? Why do they want you to behave in a certain way? What's their end-game? Sometimes you can spot the scam or an attack. Not always. But sometimes.

'How was your (online) day?': Discussing your day is something we all do. Try asking what's going on in your kids' online world too. Make talking about online life as everyday as discussing school, work and all the rest. It's amazing what you will find out.

'What are you playing?': Get to understand the games your kids are playing, with whom and how the action unfolded today. Playground politics are alive and kicking – often quite hard – in the digital world.

Social signals: Before you download a new app, look at the reviews. Be wary of apps with, say, ten glowing reviews. Could these be the developers and their friends? Look at the reviews, read them and look for patterns.

Privileges: Before you download an Android app you can read about the privileges it needs. Privileges here mean access to things like your contact database, location and the phone's cameras. Some privilege requests are quite normal and logical. A photograph app will need access to your camera. But dubious apps will ask for access to phone features way beyond reasonable. Torch apps requesting access to your contacts, for example. Avoid these apps.

Technical aids

There are a lot of different technologies to help keep us safe online. None re perfect. Here are a few of the major ones:

Firewall: A firewall is a security device that monitors Internet traffic as it flows in and out of your house. The firewall follows specific rules when deciding whether to let information flow. You are likely to have one. They are built into most broadband routers and modems. **The problem:** If you're at home and access the Internet via mobile – 4G – you will bypass your broadband firewall.

Anti–virus for your desktop: If you use a Mac or Windows PC and venture on to the Internet without antivirus software you are asking for big trouble. You really should have antivirus software. **The problem:** If you are reckless – say determined to download that £45 game for free from the Internet – you are more likely defeat your own defences. Antivirus software will often warn you if it thinks something is wrong, but if you are utterly determined to execute that –

too good to be true – download, it will let you and you will have to live with the, likely dire, consequences.

Anti–virus for your phone: Again, like your desktop PC, antivirus for your mobile is very valuable – particularly if you use Android. **The problem:** Like PC antivirus, mobile malware protection is only one component of a wider defence.

Internet filters: The big broadband providers – BT, Sky, TalkTalk, Virgin, PlusNet and EE – all offer filters that vet content. They often work on a sliding scale where you, as the parent, can set the level of explicitness that you find acceptable. These filters are well worth investigating. They are great because every device in the house – phones, tables, PCs, smart TVs – everything – is well protected. **The problem:** If your child is accessing the web via 4G from home, they'll sidestep these broadband filters. And, the filters can be a bit annoying. Set the tolerance too high and you will block access to the National Lottery's website, for example, or that wine company's free prize draw that you want to enter.

Parental controls: Many of today's major apps, operating systems and sites offer parental controls. They are

a useful way of filtering and limiting what your children can do. **The problem:** YouTube's parental settings, for example, are fallible and, what's right for one family might be wrong for another. Remember too, parental settings are just as easily disabled, as enabled.

Privacy settings: BCS has done, and continues to do, a lot of work about personal data: how we are trading information about ourselves for free access to sites like WhatsApp and Facebook. Understanding the forces at play and your family's position on privacy are, I think, important precursors to making privacy configurations in your favourite apps.

Patching: Keep all your phones, tablets, PCs and smart devices rigorously up-to-date with the manufacturer's latest software.

6 February 2018

⇨ The above information is reprinted with kind permission from The Chartered Institute for IT (BCS). Please visit www.bcs.org for further information.

© 2018 BCS

The view of young people on social media

BCS, The Chartered Institute for IT, recently conducted a survey to seek the views of young people on online safety, to coincide with the Government's consultation on its Internet Safety Strategy

75% of young people think social media companies should automatically block offensive or abusive messages

Over 40% of young people don't think digital companies consider their safety when developing websites or apps

OVER 60%
of young people think social media companies should delete abusive messages before a complaint is made

Almost 70% of young people think it would be helpful to know how much bullying happens on social media

But 50% of young people don't think knowing this would stop or change their use of the social media platforms

50% of young people want schools to teach them more about how to be safe online

TOP TRENDS

HELP

Young people are keen to receive more digital resilience education

As children get older, their desire to be shielded from abusive or offensive content on social media reduces

Young people don't think social media companies consider them, when developing apps

Young people want more information on how much antisocial content is on social media. But they will carry on using it regardless

Younger children particularly want social media platforms to remove offensive or abusive content or messages before a complaint is made

This survey was undertaken to coincide with the Government's consultation on its Internet Safety Strategy.
The survey was sent to teachers working in 1,700+ primary and secondary schools via the Computing at Schools network. They were asked to request their pupils to fill in the survey.
The survey was open from 27 November 2017 – 1 January 2018, and received 6,505 responses.

Source: bcs The Chartered Institute for IT. For more information visit bcs.org/digitalyouth

How a Digital 5 A Day can help children lead healthy online lives

By Anne Longfield

We know that the amount of time that children are online is increasing, with very young children routinely spending over 8 hours a week and 12–15-year-olds spending over 20 hours a week online. With the summer holidays in full flow, social media is often a constant presence on kids' iPads, smart phones and computers. While most parents understand that digital is just a part of life for children now, and of course many mums, dads and carers spend time online doing similar things themselves, they want to be confident that their children are living a healthy online life.

The Internet wasn't designed with children in mind, yet a third of its use is by children and they themselves tell us they see no difference between 'online life' and 'offline life'. To them, it's just 'life'. The digital world is an amazing place, but it has few rules, is vast and fast moving. I know many parents feel out of their depth or are even scared to challenge their children's use of the Internet and social media and are looking for some simple advice. That's why we are launching a new campaign called Digital 5 A Day. It is a guide for parents to help them to encourage their children to enjoy the online world without being totally consumed by it.

I don't think parents should be afraid of children's digital lives – but what they should avoid doing is allowing their children to use the Internet and social media in the same way they would use sweets or junk food given half the chance. You wouldn't let an eight-year-old eat a double cheeseburger and fries every day of the year, so it's important children aren't left to use smart phones, computers or tablets without agreed boundaries. It doesn't have to be about restriction and control – which is unlikely to win over any child anyway – but something children will often love: working out together a good way to be online.

So our 5 A Day guide promotes a positive relationship with technology rather than being too restrictive and is actually based on the NHS's five steps to mental well-being. We've placed those in a digital context and think it gives parents guidance and children room to explore and learn while keeping them safe. Importantly, it encourages them to do so themselves.

The five elements of a good digital diet are: connect, be active, get creative, give to others, be mindful.

Connect: The Internet has enabled everyone to maintain friendships and family relationships, no matter where they are in the world, and children often say that chatting with friends is the best thing about social media. It's important to acknowledge that this is how children keep in touch but it's also important to have a conversation with them about privacy settings. Remember to keep a dialogue open and talk to your child to understand how they're spending their time and so that they can come to you for help should they need to.

Be active: physical activity is very important for mental well being and all children should have time to switch off and get moving. Children don't have to be an athlete to be active. Find something that they enjoy – be that swimming, walking or dancing – and begin at a level that works for them and make it a regular activity. Researching an activity or place online before going out is a good way of combining the two and provides an opportunity for you to use the Internet together.

Get creative: The Internet provides children with unlimited opportunities to learn and to be creative. From learning to code to building complex structures in *Minecraft* to creating video content, the summer can be a great opportunity for children to grow their digital skills. Time spent online doesn't have to be spent passively consuming content. It can be educational, creative and can provide opportunities to build skills for later life.

Give to others: As well as using the Internet to learn about how to get involved with local and national charitable schemes, children can give to others through their everyday activities. Remind children that by giving positive feedback and support to friends and family as well as reporting the negative behaviour of others, children can help the web make a positive place for everyone.

Be mindful: We hear that children often feel pressured by the constantly connected nature of the Internet. While they might want to do other things, it can be difficult for them to put their phones down when apps are encouraging them to engage. Being mindful about the amount of time that your child is spending online – and encouraging them to be mindful about how this makes them feel – is important. Encourage children to come up with ways of managing this, i.e. keeping a diary as a way of logging the amount of time they are spending online or downloading an app that helps them manage their notifications.

Taken as a whole, and supplemented with parents' own ideas about what they want for their children, I hope 5 A Day will be at the very least a starting point for parents to tackle one of the modern parenting world's newest and biggest dilemmas and help children to lead the way as active digital citizens.

6 August 2017

⇨ The above information is reprinted with kind permission from The Children's Commissioner's Office. Please visit www.childrenscommissioner.gov.uk for further information.

Young people and social networking services

Social networking apps such as Facebook, Twitter, Instagram and Snapchat are very popular with young people, even those who are of primary age.

These types of services allow young people to be creative online and keep in touch with their friends, as well as share photos and videos. On some social networks, young people can follow their favourite celebrity which means they can access the content they update and share. However, for parents and carers it's important to have a look at these services either by creating your own account to try an app out, or by creating an account together with your child to familiarise you with how it works. Most services stipulate a minimum user age of 13, although some interactive services are designed specifically for younger children.

'Most sites stipulate a minimum user age of 13'

By understanding these services and their potential risks you can help to support your child in choosing an appropriate service and using it in a safe and constructive way, and be able to help them if they need it.

Many things can contribute to your child's digital footprint including what they post and who they interact with. Young people are accessing and using social networking services on a range of devices such as mobile phones, tablets and gaming devices. They use social networking services for many different purposes; to communicate with their friends, to share photos, to play games and to find out new information. You need to remind your child however that they need to be careful about what they're posting online and who can see it. Children can sometimes believe that social networking services are a private space for them and it can be difficult for them to realise that actually what they're posting online may be public and can be spread very quickly and to a large audience. The blur between public and private expression can potentially put a child at risk in two main ways:

Content

Children who create or post inappropriate, offensive or even illegal content in their own or others' pages and feeds could get themselves into trouble with their school, friends, or even break the law, depending on the nature of the material. It's also important that young people understand the longevity of posting something online.

Once content is uploaded, it could potentially stay online forever. Regardless of whether the owner takes down the content, anyone who had access to that content could have copied it for themselves, kept it for their own records or distributed it further. Content which is uploaded online can be copied, altered and reposted by anyone and it is very difficult to 'take back' things that may be later regretted. This can damage friendships/relationships, reputations and even future prospects.

Contact

Young people need to be aware that any personal information they upload could potentially reach a much wider audience than intended. If a user of a social networking service doesn't protect their information by enabling the correct privacy settings, they could be exposing their information to strangers and as a result be at risk of online contact and grooming. Posting or chatting about personal details might enable someone to identify and contact your child online or in person. There is also the more likely risk of cyberbullying with young people intentionally harming another person online. Talk to your child about why protecting their privacy online is important and talk through the available privacy settings with them.

It's a good idea to talk to your child about their social networking life online. In the same way that you might ask them about their social life offline, talking about social networking services together is no different. Why not start with a positive conversation about what they like to do online, and why they like the services that they use? You can then ask them whether they know where to go for help, or whether they know how to make their profile private, or even ask them to help you with your privacy settings.

Privacy settings

These settings give the user the ability to control who they share particular content with, for example making a photo you post visible to friends only or to the public. Encourage children and young people to use the privacy tools available on the social networking service to protect their personal information and to keep their passwords private (even from their friends). Information on how to do this can be found at www.saferinternet.org.uk/checklists. Most social networking sites give safety advice and information on their safety tools. Links to this advice and information can be found at www.saferinternet.org.uk/safety-tools.

Online friendship

Remind your child to consider carefully who they add as friends or followers, and what those friends and followers can see once added to a contact list. Your most trustworthy online friends are the people you also know and trust offline.

Geolocation

Young people must be aware of who they are sharing their location with. If they are accessing a social networking service via a smartphone or mobile device, they might be disclosing their location without realising it. Location services can be turned on or off per app within the settings of a device.

Think before you post

Emphasise the importance of thinking before you post something online. This can include writing a comment or sharing a picture. It can also include sharing on things that others have posted. Discuss with them what is and isn't OK to say in a post and remind them that sometimes messages online can be misunderstood. What may start out as a harmless joke for one person can be extremely hurtful for another individual and once something is posted online it is potentially there forever. If you are not sure, or if you wouldn't be happy for your Head Teacher to see it, it's probably best not to post it. Your online reputation can also be affected by other behaviour, such as groups you join or clicking 'likes'.

Consider the photos you upload

It's important that children consider the content of the images they share online, and the impact they may have on their own reputation, and the emotions of others. They should always ensure that they ask permission from others before posting pictures of them online.

Know how to block and report

Make sure children and young people know how to report abusive comments or illegal activity on social networking services. Many social networking sites allow you to report a comment or user who is potentially breaking their terms and conditions, by clicking on a report button or filling out an online form. If young people have concerns about cyberbullying then they should speak to a trusted adult as well as save the evidence, and use the tools available to block other users. If you have concerns that your child is or has been the subject of inappropriate sexual contact or approach by another person, it's vital that you report it to the police via the Child Exploitation and Online Protection Centre (www. ceop.police.uk).

Security

Make sure your child chooses a strong password, avoiding identifiable words

or phrases such as birthdays and pets names. A good password should also include a mixture of upper and lower case letters, numbers and symbols. Once your child has finished using a social networking service it is important for them to log out, especially when using a public or shared computer. Make sure they have locked their mobile device with a pin or password, as mislaid devices can mean that others could access their social networking accounts.

2018

⇨ The above information has been taken from a Childnet resource *Young People and Social Networking Services* with kind permission from Childnet International. Please visit www.childnet.com for further information and the full resource.

#StatusOfMind

Social media and young people's mental health and well-being.

Key points

⇨ 91% of 16–24-year-olds use the Internet for social networking.

⇨ Social media has been described as more addictive than cigarettes and alcohol.

⇨ Rates of anxiety and depression in young people have risen 70% in the past 25 years.

⇨ Social media use is linked with increased rates of anxiety, depression and poor sleep.

⇨ Cyberbullying is a growing problem with seven in ten young people saying they have experienced it.

⇨ Social media can improve young people's access to other people's experiences of health and expert health information.

⇨ Those who use social media report being more emotionally supported through their contacts.

91% of 16–24-year-olds use the Internet for social media

The way young people communicate and share with each other has changed. With social media being such a new phenomenon, the exact effect it is having on the mental health, emotional well-being and physiology of young people is currently unclear

and much of the evidence available is conflicting. However, recent studies have raised serious concerns about the possible detrimental effects the rise of increasingly frequent social media use is having on our young people – and in particular, their mental health.

Adolescence and early adulthood is a critical and potentially vulnerable time

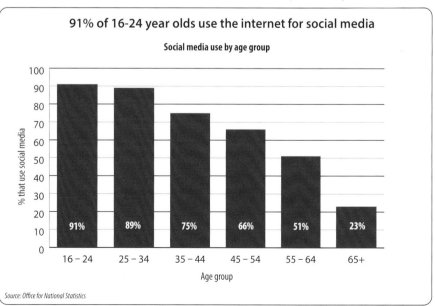

91% of 16-24 year olds use the internet for social media

Social media use by age group

Source: Office for National Statistics

for social and emotional development, which means understanding the effects of social media on health at this stage is of particular interest. This report explores both the positive and negative impacts social media, identified by expert academics, may be having on young people's mental health and emotional well-being, and suggests ways in which the risks to health can be mitigated, whilst harnessing and promoting the positive aspects. Social media can and should be utilised as a tool for good – the challenge is to ensure social media companies are doing their utmost to make platforms a safe place to be, and for our young people to be equipped with the relevant skills to be able to navigate them and know where to seek help, should they need it.

What is RSPH calling for?

1. The introduction of a pop-up heavy usage warning on social media

The social media platform would track usage and provide the user with a pop-up warning when they breach a set level of usage deemed potentially harmful. It is then up to the user to decide if they carry on using the platform or stop, although the warning may provide links to information and advice on social media addiction.

The evidence is clear that increased use of social media can be detrimental to some aspects of the health and well-being of young people. As with other potentially harmful practices, those partaking in them should be informed of the potential consequences before making their own decision on their actions. A pop-up warning would give young people access to this information so they can make informed decisions about their own health.

Some young people would like to see this go further with almost one-third (30%) of the young people who completed our survey supporting the idea of a heavy usage cap, whereby individuals would be automatically logged out of social media if they breached a set level of usage.

2. Social media platforms to highlight when photos of people have been digitally manipulated

This may be in the form of a small icon or watermark at the bottom of someone's photo that indicates an airbrush or filter has been used that may have significantly altered their appearance.

Young people, and in particular young women, are bombarded with images that attempt to pass off the edited as the norm. This practice is contributing to a generation of young people with poor body image and body confidence. Fashion brands, celebrities and other advertising organisations may sign up to a voluntary code of practice where the small icon is displayed on their photos to indicate an image may have been digitally enhanced or altered to significantly alter the appearance of people in it

3. NHS England to apply the Information Standard Principles to health information published via social media

The sheer volume of health information that is now available on social media means that it may be difficult for young people to know which sources they can trust and get reliable and consistent information from. This is especially the case with the emergence of so-called 'fake news', meaning trust is declining in information on social media platforms.

The Information Standard is a certification scheme that lets the public know an organisation that is giving out information on health and social care is trustworthy. We would like to see NHS England apply this same quality filter to health information that is published on social media platforms.

4. Safe social media use to be taught during PSHE education in school

RSPH has long called for the introduction of comprehensive, statutory Personal, Social and Health Education (PSHE) in schools. A component of this education should feature the safe use of social media including: cyber bullying and where to seek help; social media addiction; body image and social media, and

other potential effects of social media on mental health. The education system must evolve with the society in which it operates and equip our young people with the tools necessary to navigate the digital age in a way which protects their mental health and emotional wellbeing.

5. Social media platforms to identify users who could be suffering from mental health problems by their posts and other data, and discreetly signpost to support

If social media is contributing to poor mental health in young people we should be utilising the various platforms to reach and help those who are suffering. The existing stigma around mental health issues, particularly in young people, may make it difficult for those suffering to come forward or even know where to look for help. We would like to see technology used to identify those young people who could be suffering from mental health conditions on social media, and provide them with discreet information about where they can find help and advice should they wish to receive it.

6. Youth-workers and other professionals who engage with young people to have a digital (including social) media component in their training

Digital technologies, including social media, are so entrenched in the lives of young people that it is no longer possible to support the health and well-being of young people without some knowledge regarding the impact these technologies and social media platforms have. If we are to promote the positive aspects of social media, those who have frequent contact with young people should be trained accordingly.

Online toolkits, such as those provided by Aye Mind, can offer digital resources for adults working with young people and help them understand the possible risks and potential for good that social media and the online world offers. Although many adults are themselves on social media, the nature of being a young person means the challenges faced online are different, so it is important adults working with young people are kept up-to-date on the changing landscape of online communication and social networking.

7. More research to be carried out into the effects of social media on young people's mental health

The emerging evidence available to us is suggesting that there may be some significant risks posed by social media use to young people's mental health and emotional wellbeing. However, research is thus far limited and due to social media being a relatively new introduction to the lives of young people, far more long-term research will be necessary before we are able to fully understand its effects. We would like to see academic institutions, independent researchers and social media companies fund and undertake much more research into the subject.

2017

Digital footprints

What are digital footprints and how do they affect an online reputation?

We have all heard of the term 'digital footprints' but do we really understand what it means? It is important that parents and carers do understand what these footprints are so that they can in turn educate their children and help them to know what risks they might be placing themselves in when sharing information online, or just looking innocently at websites.

Whatever we are doing on the Internet we can leave a trail of information behind us which people can use to determine what we might be interested in buying, or for other less savoury purposes such as trying to hack into our online accounts and trying to access passwords, etc.

So what is a digital footprint?

A digital footprint is data that is left behind when users have been online. There are two types of digital footprints which are passive and active. A passive footprint is made when information is collected from the user without the person knowing this is happening. An active digital footprint is where the user has deliberately shared information about themselves either by using social media sites or by using websites.

An example of a passive digital footprint would be where a user has been online and information has been stored on an online database. This can include where they came from, when the footprint was created and a user IP address. A footprint can also be analysed offline and can be stored in files which an administrator can access.

These would include information on what that machine might have been used for, but not who had performed the actions.

An example of an active digital footprint is where a user might have logged into a site when editing or making comments such as on an online forum or a social media site. The registered name or profile can be linked to the posts that have been made and it is surprisingly easy to find out a lot about a person from the trails you leave behind.

Web browsing and digital footprints

The digital footprint we leave after browsing websites is called the Internet footprint. These are commonly called 'cookies' and most websites will ask you to accept the use of cookies before you can access the site, without actually knowing what this means. If we inadvertently leave a lot of information about ourselves behind it could be passively or actively collected by other people just by using a simple search engine.

It is becoming more and more common for employers to 'cyber vet' prospective employees based on their online activities. Digital footprints can also be used by the police to gather information about individuals to help them with their enquiries.

Social networking sites can also give a very good idea of an individual's life. These sites can allow digital tracing data which can include what social groups they belong to, their interests, location, etc. This data can be gathered and analysed without the users being aware that this is happening.

A lot of employers will also use social media to vet prospective employees so it is important that you are mindful as to what you post on any such sites. Of course there is no limit as to how far you can go back in time on social media sites and once something is posted, there is no way of removing it completely. Others might have commented or shared your posts and this in turn will create their own digital footprint. This is something that needs to be discussed with your children and teenagers so they can be educated and are aware what might happen to that information.

So how much privacy do we really have?

Digital footprints including the meta data and content does impact on security, privacy and trust. As the Internet becomes bigger and bigger it is becoming increasingly important to think about what might happen to the ownership of the photos that you own and content that you write. Remember that what goes on the internet normally stays there, even if you do delete posts there will be a trail of data that you have left behind.

Talking to your child or teen

⇨ Have a chat with them when you know they are using social media sites, or on the Internet.

⇨ Let them know what is expected of them and what is a 'no go'.

⇨ Explain the dangers of posting content that you feel might be inappropriate or controversial and the trail that can be left behind.

⇨ Ensure that they know the dangers of posting content and personal details, including pictures.

⇨ Encourage them not to divulge any personal details such as age, address or contact details to anyone online.

⇨ If they feel they might have put themselves in danger, or feel in danger, remember to reassure them that you are always there to support them.

⇨ Many people want to share the fact that they are going on holiday and how long they are going for – think about the impact and danger this could be placing your family in.

⇨ It is a criminal offence to use the Internet to threaten or harass people.

⇨ The above information is reprinted with kind permission from Family Lives. Please visit www.familylives. org.uk for further information.

© 2018 Family Lives

What information shouldn't you post on social media?

We reveal what the dangers of oversharing on social media are.

By Kyri Levendi

You get access to a lot of information on your social media newsfeed. In one quick swipe, you can see who's celebrating their birthday, holidaying on the other side of the world or moving into a new home.

But there is such a thing as oversharing. Especially, as fraudsters are using social media more and more to piece together your information and use it to commit identity fraud.

To help you protect your personal information, we explain the details you should never give out on social media.

Don't include personal information in your username

You have to come up with a unique username on sites like Twitter and Instagram. When doing this, make sure you pick one that doesn't reveal too much about yourself.

For example, 'JohnSmith_Manchester' or 'Claire.Smith.London' might not be the best idea, as it reveals too much personal information.

Be careful about the information you share

You might think that it's harmless to include your full name, date of birth and where you live on your social media – but think again.

This information is the first thing a fraudster will use to try to guess your passwords. To be on the safe side, try to limit how much information you give out. And if you still want to get birthday messages, simply remove the year you were born.

Only connect with people you know

It can be flattering to accept friend requests from old work colleagues or high-school friends. But do you really want people that you haven't spoken to in years to have access to your personal information?

It can be wise to have a regular clear out of friends or followers on social media. You don't even have to block or delete people, just change your settings to limit the amount of access they have to your profile.

Your profile should be private to the general public as well, so only your friends and followers have full access to it.

Think twice about what you post

We know this might seem obvious, but you should never post pictures of your credit card, bill or new driving licence on social media.

You'll not only give your followers access to your full name and address, but sensitive information like your account number as well. While, fraudsters won't be able to use this information by itself to gain access to your finances, it could help them build up a clearer picture of your identity.

2 November 2017

⇨ The above information is reprinted with kind permission from Think Money. Please visit www. thinkmoney.co.uk for further information.

© 2018 Think Money

How can we stop social media undermining our mental health?

Rather than asking if social media is the problem, let's for a moment ask what the screen reflects. Our desire to capture and communicate a positive identity has always existed. Keeping diaries was all the rage for millions of our Victorian-era predecessors. Social media is the latest manifestation.

By Cal Strode

Social media is something we brought into existence, not something that happened to us. Its skeleton is a vast network of algorithms, built to reflect and take advantage of our desires and behaviours.

One of these behaviours – social comparison – was captured perfectly in 1913, when a US comic strip coined the phrase 'keeping up with the Joneses'. The comic resonated with millions of Americans, capturing the anxiety and misery of looking over the fence to our neighbours for comparison and benchmarks for success.

Today we can see far beyond that fence. The average Facebook user can see into the lives of 338 friends. Naturally, we're starting to wonder if our expanded line of sight could be having a negative impact on our mental health.

What we do know, is that self-acceptance and self-esteem are crucial for good mental health. Comparing ourselves to others, be it online or offline, can undermine these things, giving rise to feelings of inadequacy.

One study suggests that whether or not comparing ourselves to others online can harm us depends on a number of factors, namely:

⇨ the degree to which we are comparing ourselves to what we see on our feeds, and the amount of time we spend doing it.

⇨ the degree to which we believe what we see is an accurate portrayal of reality.

⇨ the degree of perceived similarity between ourselves and the people we're comparing ourselves to.

Based on this, then, online comparison could be particularly harmful if we spend a lot of time comparing our lives to the highlights of our friends' lives. To try to reduce the impact of these three factors in our own lives, there are a couple of things we could try.

The first challenge will be catching those unconscious moments when we slip into comparison mode. We could try to be more intentional with the time we spend on social media. Deleting mobile apps and logging into desktop versions while getting into this habit could help. Often, we can unconsciously open our phones and start scrolling through our feeds, regaining consciousness ten minutes into comparing ourselves to our feeds!

We could also seek out more life-affirming content that reflects the behind the scenes of our realities. This could help to minimise the alienating impact of seeing nothing but highlights. There are tons of social media groups based on a range of things we will recognise from our own lives, including mental health peer support groups and communities.

For the final similarity factor, it might be worth thinking about who, from our social feeds, we feel most in competition with. Are there any particular names that come to mind that maybe trigger feelings of insecurity? Consider un-following them for a while on apps where this is possible. It's not the same as unfriending so they wont know, it just means you won't see them in your feed for a while.

By moving beyond asking if social media is the problem, and starting to dissect the root problems it could be reflecting to us, maybe we can minimise the opportunity social media has to undermine our mental health.

2 February 2018

⇨ The above information is reprinted with kind permission from Mental Health Foundation. Please visit www.mentalhealth.org.uk for further information.

Social media bad for mental health? Not in my view!

By Natasha Fineron

Earlier this week the media reported new stats that showed the number of women seeking help for self-harm has doubled in the last 20 years – sparking a debate on the impact of social media on our mental health. We asked Natalya, one of our young champions to tell us her view and to share her tips for staying well online.

For most people, self-harm is a secretive activity – often as a result of being unable to express your emotions in a healthy way, or to feel in control of something when you feel helpless. Often, family and friends will be unaware that this is happening, and it is easy for those feelings of isolation and loneliness to increase and add to that vicious cycle.

Social media can offer a safe space to talk and express that pent-up frustration. While I do not dispute that social media can have an incredibly negative impact on people, and that how society and the media tells girls they should look is still a massive issue, we often neglect to highlight how important social media can be for those who are otherwise isolated or unable to talk to anyone. It can be potentially life-saving.

We know that the ability to be anonymous can be a huge problem with social media, giving people the capability to insult and abuse with complete freedom. But that anonymity can also provide a safe haven for people who would otherwise be too scared to talk about what they're going through.

When I first started self–harming at 16, I had a Tumblr blog and I would use it to vent and journal my feelings. I would also use it to connect and find advice from people who were going through or had gone through the same thing as me. It made me feel less alone. Obviously, there were dangers with that – a platform that allows people to express themselves fully also means that people can express unhealthy ways of thinking and patterns of behaviour that could be triggering, and you do have to be wary of that.

> **"I believe that teenagers are far more switched on to the issues with excessive social media usage than we give them credit for – they have grown up in the age of social media after all."**

We must consider the fact that social media is rarely the cause of mental illness – rather it is the societal pressures of school/money/parents/friendships/job prospects that can negatively affect young people. Yes, these things are also present on social media, but social media is only a reflection of society. We can't say that social media is the problem, without also acknowledging that society as a whole is a problem. Social media just amplifies that.

As ever, nothing is black and white, and rarely are things ever only good or bad. Talk to your children, your peers or your parents about social media, discuss potential issues but also discuss the things you find helpful about it. Discuss how to keep yourself safe and how to keep yourself healthy. It's OK if you slip up or struggle, but talking, whether in person or online, will help, I know that from my own experiences.

My tips for using social media in a healthy manner:

⇨ If you feel that it is negatively affecting your life, talk to someone about it – a friend, a therapist, a parent. Turn off when you can and mute your notifications – don't let social media overwhelm you.

⇨ Enforce your boundaries – mute topics which you find distressing, unfollow people who make you feel bad about yourself, don't feel like you have to answer messages or play snapchats immediately. Give yourself a break if you need to. If people make you feel bad about that, they are not worth your time.

⇨ You don't have to read every bit of news. You don't need to be up to date with exactly what's going on the world. Try not to endlessly scroll through hundreds and hundreds of updates!

⇨ Finally, remember that social media is a skewed view of life, people like to upload the perfect photos and updates about their lives – censoring out the bad bits. Most people's lives are not that perfect so don't compare yourself.

11 August 2018

⇨ The above information is reprinted with kind permission from Rethink Mental Illness. Please visit www.rethink.org for further information.

A 'Goldilocks amount of screen time' might be good for teenagers' well-being

Says lead author Dr Andrew Przybylski, of the Oxford Internet Institute at the University of Oxford

A new study argues that while a lot has been said by scientists and paediatricians about the possible dangers of teenagers spending time on digital devices or computers, there is little robust evidence to back up their claims. The researchers say they are the first to systematically test for links between well-being and screen time measured continuously, separately for different digital activities and days of the week. They have proposed the Goldilocks theory: that there is a point between low and high use of technology that is 'just right' for teenagers when their sense of well-being is boosted by having 'moderate' amounts of screen time. The researchers suggest this may be because digital connectivity can enhance creativity, communication skills and development. Their findings also suggest that the relationship between screen time and well-being is weak at best, even when young people overuse their digital devices. The paper is published in the journal, *Psychological Science*.

Using a well-established self-report measure of mental well-being, researchers from Oxford and Cardiff universities analysed how 120,000 15-year-olds in Britain felt after using digital technology and how much time they spent on different devices. Nearly all (99.9%) of the participating adolescents reported spending time using at least one type of digital technology on a daily basis. The teenagers were asked about time spent watching films and TV programmes, playing computer games, using the Internet, or smartphones for social networking and chatting. The paper concludes that more than 'moderate' time can be linked with a negative effect on well–being, but they estimate this is a 'small' effect at 1% or less – equivalent to one-third of the positive effect on well-being of a good night's sleep or regularly eating breakfast.

The researchers tested their digital Goldilocks hypothesis against the data, finding that teenagers' well-being increased as their screen time increased, up to a certain point. After that point, increased screen time was associated with decreased well-being. The study also highlights that the point at which screen times flipped between moderate and potentially harmful screen time were notably at higher amounts and less variable for days at the weekend. The research finds that moderate digital activity does not generally displace other activities essential for mental well-being; however, smartphones at the weekend could be harmful if a virtual social life disrupted other more rewarding social activities that could have taken place in a teenager's free time.

Thresholds defining the point at which 'moderate' use becomes overuse and affects well-being negatively varied according to the digital device and whether teenagers played during the week or at weekends, says the study. It suggests time should be limited to one hour 40 minutes for weekday video-game play and one hour 57 minutes for weekday smartphone use. Watching videos and using

1 hour   2 hours   3 hours   4 hours

computers for recreational purposes appears to be less disruptive so limits during the weekdays were three hours 41 minutes and four hours 17 minutes, respectively. For weekends, the limit was three hours 35 minutes for playing video games to four hours 50 minutes for watching videos. The authors speculate that 'moderate' levels of digital screen use are lower on weekdays because the weekdays are relatively richer in opportunities for socialising and learning compared to weekends.

Lead author Dr Andrew Przybylski, of the Oxford Internet Institute at the University of Oxford, said: 'Previous research has oversimplified the relationship between digital screen time and the mental well-being of teenagers. Overall we found that modern use of digital technology is not intrinsically harmful and may have advantages in a connected world unless digital devices are overused or interfere with schoolwork or afterschool activities. Our research suggests that some connectivity is probably better than none and there are moderate levels that, as in the story of Goldilocks, are 'just right' for young people.'

Co-author Dr Netta Weinstein of Cardiff University commented: 'To the extent that digital activities either enrich teenagers' lives or displace more rewarding activities, they should have either positive or negative effects on their mental well-being. There have been theories that digital use is disrupting more satisfying pursuits. However, the role of digital technology has a central role in everyday life and online gaming is now a shared way of playing for teenage boys. There is good reason to think digital technology used in moderation is not disruptive and may even support development.'

13 January 2017

⇨ The above information is reprinted with kind permission from University of Oxford. Please visit www.ox.ac.uk for further information.

What is cyberbullying?

Cyberbullying is any form of bullying that is carried out through the use of electronic media devices, such as computers, laptops, smartphones, tablets or gaming consoles

What makes cyberbullying different?

We know there is a strong link between cyberbullying and face-to-face bullying. Research has shown that 80% of victims of cyberbullying were also bullied face to face.

"Bullying is far more widespread now it is online – it's not just your time in school. It affects your social life. Your social life is online. How many people like your status or your picture. Social pressures are just made worse."

There are some things that make cyberbullying different to 'traditional' bullying:

⇨ 24-7 nature – the nature of online activity means you can be in contact at any time.

⇨ There is the potential for a wider audience and bullying incidents can stay online, for example: a photo that you can't remove

⇨ Evidence – a lot of cyberbullying incidents allow those experiencing it to keep evidence – for example, take a screen shot – to show to school staff or police if needed.

⇨ Potential to hide your identity – it is possible to hide your identity online which can make cyberbullying incidents very scary

⇨ Degree of separation – people who cyberbully often don't see the reaction of those experiencing it so it can sometimes be harder for them to see the impact of their actions

Prevalence of cyberbullying

There are many statistics relating to levels of cyberbullying. In the briefing in the Tools and Research section on our website you will see our Focus On briefing which outlines current research on bullying including (please see briefing for references):

⇨ 24% of children and young people will experience some form of cyberbullying

⇨ 17% of children and young people will cyberbully others

⇨ Name calling is the most common type of cyberbullying.

17 April 2017

⇨ The above information is reprinted with kind permission from Anti-Bullying Alliance. Please visit www.anti-bullyingalliance.org.uk for further information.

What to do if you're being bullied on a social network

Bullying on Facebook, Twitter, YouTube, WhatsApp, Instagram and Snapchat.

With the increase of social networking sites, online activity and messaging apps, cyberbullying is on the increase. In a survey by Ditch the Label, 47% of young people who took the survey have received nasty profile comments and 62% have been sent nasty private messages via smartphone apps. This is very worrying as it shows how cyberbullying is on the increase.

Most of the apps and social networking sites are for people aged 13 and over. They also state that bullying and abusive behaviours, which include harassment, impersonation and identity theft are banned and not allowed. However, results from our national bullying survey, shows 91% of people who reported cyberbullying said that no action was taken. This can leave users feeling disbelieved, vulnerable and knock their self-esteem.

A general rule when making a complaint about being bullied online is to copy the terms and conditions that have been breached and take a screenshot of the comment or photo as evidence. This may prompt any of these sites and apps to take action as you have shown them their obligation to investigate and take appropriate action.

How to report bullying or abuse on social media

Facebook

Facebook does not tolerate bullying and say they will remove bullying content when they become aware of it and may disable the account of anyone who bullies or attacks another. They have a set of community standards that they adhere to and it states that they will not tolerate:

⇨ Pages that identify and shame private individuals,

⇨ Images altered to degrade private individuals,

⇨ Photos or videos of physical bullying posted to shame the victim,

⇨ Sharing personal information to blackmail or harass people, and

⇨ Repeatedly targeting other people with unwanted friend requests or messages.

You can report bullying on Facebook using the report links which appear near the content itself, normally on a drop down arrow which gives you menu option to report the image, post or comment.

Twitter

If you receive a tweet or reply that you don't like, you can unfollow that person. If they continue to contact you, you can block the user (just click on the head icon on their profile and select block user). You may find that as they are unable to get through to you, they will lose interest. However, if this is not the case and you continue to receive unwanted replies, abuse or threats, you can report it to Twitter directly. If you know a friend or family member is being abused on Twitter, they have advice pages that can help with step-by-step help.

YouTube

You have every right to use YouTube without fear of being subjected to bullying or harassment. Bullying can be reported and action taken when things cross a line. To flag a video you think is inappropriate (click on the little flag bottom right of the video) and YouTube will take a look at it to see whether it breaks their terms of use. If it does then they will remove it. YouTube rules say you can't upload videos with hate content, nudity or graphic violence and if you find one on someone else's space, click on the video to flag it as inappropriate. If under comments, you are being bullied, harassed or threats are being made, they have a reporting tool page where you can report the bullying and they will investigate.

How to report bullying or abuse on messaging apps

Instagram

Bullying or abuse on Instagram can happen in many ways. It can be either negative comments, fake profiles or hacking of accounts. Instagram take all of these violations very seriously and have plenty of advice on their pages if you or someone you know is being bullied or abused on Instagram. Their advice initially is to block and unfollow the person who is being abusive. However, if it continues or it has gotten worse, you can use their in-app reporting tool.

Snapchat

Snapchat is an app that allows users to send pictures to each other that disappear off screen within a set amount of time. Unfortunately, there is bullying on Snapchat in the form of screenshots, sending pics without permission, negative comments and more. If this is the case for you or someone you know they can block a user, tap the Menu icon, select 'My Friends', locate their name in the list and swipe right across their name. If you would like to delete a friend from your contacts, press 'Delete'. Even if you haven't added the user as a friend, their name will still appear in the 'My Friends' list under 'Recent' if they have sent you a message recently. If you receive an inappropriate photo or someone's harassing or bullying you, report it by filling out their online form.

WhatsApp

WhatsApp Messenger lets people sends instant messages, videos, photos and short audio messages to either one person or within a group chat. Messages can only be sent to other smartphone users who also have WhatsApp. Once you install the app, it checks your address book to see if anyone else you know is already using WhatsApp, and connects you automatically. You have to be over 16 to use WhatsApp legally. Bullying can take many forms as it is a messaging service and we often hear of abusive group chats. You can block and delete the contact. You can find out more by emailing them at support@whatsapp.com.

General safety tips

Keep it private

Don't post anything on a social networking site which gives your real name, address, school, phone number or which will allow a stranger to contact you in real life. Make sure you don't ID your friends either.

Don't upload anything that might embarrass you at a later date. You might not realise it but things you post on the Internet now could come back to cause problems for you later on, for instance when you go for an interview for college or a job. So if you are not happy for it to be shown to the world then do not hit send. Remember once you send it you have lost control of that image or comment.

If you have a webcam or smartphone never be pressured into taking pictures of yourself that you wouldn't want other people to see. Trust your gut instinct over this. Once again, once you hit send, you have lost control over that picture and this can cause anxiety and stress.

If you're using a shared computer at school, in an Internet cafe or library then you'll stay logged on even when you close the browser. So don't forget to log off when you've finished the session. Read more tips about staying safe online.

Protecting your tweets

On Twitter you can choose to protect your tweets so that people can only follow you if you approve them first. You can select this by going into the 'Settings menu' then 'Security and Privacy' and ticking the box for 'protect my tweets'. Find out more about the difference on Twitter between public and protected tweets.

Location settings

Many social networks like Facebook and Twitter allow you to post your location or check in each time you tweet or post a status update. This

might seem like fun for your friends to know where you are, but it can also mean that people you don't know will see where you are, especially if you're tweeting from your mobile on a profile that is public. To turn off the location settings, go into the 'Settings' menu, scroll down 'Security and Privacy' then to 'Tweet Location' and untick the checkbox that says 'Add a location to my tweets'. You can also press the button that says 'Delete all location data', to clear information about where you've been in the past.

Snapchat has developed a new feature called Snap Map which can show your location. It is very important to turn this feature off so you are able to keep safe. Snap Map tracks your current location and places your avatar on a map like a pin. This can allow others to zoom in and find exactly where you are. It doesn't take effect until you update the app, and it has an opt-out option. If you're opening the app for the first time after the update, Snapchat will walk you through a step-by-step tutorial on how to use the Snap Map. First, it'll show you how to pinch and zoom in the camera tool to access the map. Then, it'll ask who you want to see your location. You get three choices: all your friends, select

friends, or only me. Choosing 'only me' activates what it calls 'ghost mode' meaning you can see others but they can't see you. To turn off location data altogether, you'll need to visit your phone's settings where you can scroll down to Snapchat, click on 'location', and choose to never share.

Hashtags

Be wary of using hashtags as that can open up your post to be visible on that particular hashtag thread on any social network or app. It can open up your post and your account to a wider audience than you originally intended.

Inappropriate behaviour

If anyone makes you feel uncomfortable or embarrassed online then please tell your parents or someone that can help. If they're doing it to you then they might also be doing it to other people. It's particularly important never to meet up with anyone you meet online in real life, if anyone suggests that to you and particularly if they suggest you keep it secret that's a real danger sign.

When you go into a social networking site people might approach you to be a friend but remember that no matter how much they tell you about themselves, they are still strangers and they might not be telling you the truth about themselves. There have been cases of adults pretending to be young people to chat to them online and try and involve you in inappropriate activities. This is called grooming and is a criminal offence. CEOP (the Child Exploitation and Online Protection Centre) investigates cases of sex abuse and grooming on the Internet. Incidents can be reported by clicking the red button on the top right-hand corner of the CEOP website.

Although the police can get information from your computer's hard drive, it's helpful if you don't delete anything you think is dodgy until the police have decided whether they need it as evidence.

Removing or blocking friends

Facebook – click on their profile, then on the 'message' button dropdown and you will see the option to 'unfriend'. You can also block a person this way.

Twitter – to remove or block someone on Twitter, click on the button with a head icon on it next to the 'Follow' button on a user's profile. If you click on this you will see a menu with the options to BLOCK the user to prevent them from seeing your profile, and vice versa, and you can also REPORT FOR SPAM, which will alert Twitter to any users who are abusing the service.

YouTube – go to your account page and click on 'All Contacts' link in the 'Friends and Contacts' section. Choose which person you want to unfriend and the click on 'Remove Contacts'. From then on the person won't be on your 'Share Video' list.

WhatsApp – You can click on the name and then you will be taken to a dropdown menu and you can then choose to block the person.

Snapchat – to block a user who added you follow the steps below. Tap 'Added Me' on the Profile Screen. Then tap their name, and tap the wheel icon next to their name. Press 'Block' to prevent them from sending you Snaps, Chats, or from viewing your Stories.

Instagram – when you block someone, they can't see your profile or posts. People aren't notified when you block them. To block or unblock

someone, tap their username to open their profile and then tap the three dots and press the option to block user.

Closing your account

Facebook – to deactivate your Facebook account go to the 'settings' tab on the Account page. That will remove your profile and content and nobody will be able to see your details or search for you. But if you decide to reinstate the account later then the whole lot will be restored, including your friends and photos. If you would like to permanently delete your Facebook account, log in to your account, click 'Privacy and Settings', 'See More Settings' and select 'Delete my account'. Once you have confirmed your wish to delete your Facebook account it can take up to 14 days for it to happen.

Twitter – on the settings tab on your profile, you will see 'deactivate my account' at the bottom. Click on this to delete your account. You have 30 days to change your mind otherwise your profile, all of your tweets and data will be permanently deleted.

YouTube – click on 'My Account' in the top right hand corner and under 'Account Settings' click on 'Delete Account'. Give the reason you're quitting the site and your password and then click 'Delete My Account'. Log out by clicking the link in the top right-hand corner. Your videos will be removed from the site immediately and the thumbnails will disappear as soon as YouTube is updated. Your profile is removed permanently.

WhatsApp – you can remove the app from your smartphone either through app management in settings or by going into the settings of WhatsApp.

Snapchat – Open the Snapchat app, login and tap the 'Settings' icon in the upper right corner. Navigate to 'Support' and then 'Learning the Basics' and then click on delete an account.

Instagram – Log into Instagram from a mobile browser or computer. You can't temporarily disable your account from within the Instagram app. Click your username in the top right and then select 'Edit Profile'. Click temporarily disable my account

in the bottom right and follow the on-screen instructions. If you want to delete your account permanently, go to the 'Delete Your Account' page. If you're not logged into Instagram on the web, you'll be asked to log in first. Select an option from the drop-down menu next to 'Why are you deleting your account?' And re-enter your password. The option to permanently delete your account will only appear after you've selected a reason from the menu. Click or tap 'Permanently delete my account'.

Don't get into an argument or post offensive material

Don't get into arguments online, this is called flaming and it can get nasty. If you break the rules of whichever site you're on then the content is likely to be removed and you might have your membership terminated. You're not allowed to upload anything which is offensive or racist and which promotes physical harm so don't make threats to anyone. Neither are you allowed to harass people or to encourage other people to harass them. You're not supposed to ask for personal information from anyone under 18 either so if you are under 18 and anyone asks you, for instance, where you go to school, make sure you report them.

Spreading rumours

Don't spread rumours or make up false things about a friend you have fallen out with. You are not allowed to upload anything which is threatening, abusive or which is defamatory. It's defamatory if you say untrue things about someone which give them a bad reputation they don't deserve. It can also be harassment which is a criminal offence in the UK.

You're not supposed to upload a picture or video of anyone without their permission either. So never set up a social networking website account in the names of other people or upload false information about them.

⇨ The above information is reprinted with kind permission from Family Lives. Please visit www.bullying.co.uk for further information.

© 2018 Family Lives

Scroll Free September aims to wean us off social media

Take back control, urges public health body, as it encourages people to abstain or cut down.

By Denis Campbell, Health Policy Editor

We've got Dry January for anyone tempted to try alcohol abstinence and Stoptober for smokers who want to quit. Now, Scroll Free September will target the use of social media.

The Royal Society for Public Health, which is behind the campaign, is urging everyone to stop using – or reduce use of – Facebook, Twitter, Snapchat, Instagram and other social media platforms for the month.

The campaign is being billed as an 'opportunity to take back control of our relationship with social media' for the millions of Britons for whom social media plays a large, possibly unhealthily large, role in their lives.

Anyone accepting the challenge can either go cold turkey, abstaining completely for a month, or commit to reduce their use, for example by steering clear of social media at social events or in the evening.

Polling for the RSPH undertaken by Populus found that, in a representative sample of 2,057 adults, 65% would consider taking part. Significant minorities think ditching social media for a month would benefit their sleep (33%), real world relationships (33%) and general mental health and well-being (31%), with 18- to 34-year-olds the most likely to believe that.

Shirley Cramer, chief executive of the Royal Society for Public Health, said: 'The aim is that by the end of the month we will be able to reflect back on what we missed and what we got to enjoy instead of scrolling through our newsfeeds.'

But, she added: 'Of course we know this will be a challenge because of the addictive nature of social media technology.'

Chris Elmore, chair of an all-party group of MPs and peers looking at the impact of social media on young people's mental health, said: 'Many of us are becoming consumed by social media and whilst there are many benefits to using the various platforms available, it's important to take some time out.'

Almost half (45%) of those polled said taking a break would make them more productive, while 40% of those aged 18–34 thought doing so would improve their body confidence and self-esteem.

Mark Winstanley, the chief executive of Rethink Mental Illness, said people should limit, rather than abandon, their use of social media.

'Social media, like fire, can be a great servant but a deadly master,' he said. 'There's plenty of evidence that shows that those affected by mental illness can get support and guidance through social media but at the same time it can prove addictive and affect some people's well-being.'

27 July 2018

⇨ The above information is reprinted with kind permission from *The Guardian*. Please visit www.theguardian.com for further information.

Social media users are being encouraged to cut out some of their favourite platforms for 'Scroll Free September'

Those behind the campaign hope it will help improve people's mental health and well-being.

By Florence Snead

Social media users are being called to cut out some of their key platforms as part of a month–long campaign kicking off tomorrow.

The 'Scroll Free September' initiative is being spearheaded by the Royal Society for Public Health (RSPH) in the hope it will improve people's mental health and well-being.

Those taking part in the campaign can still use platforms such as Twitter and Facebook for work purposes but are encouraged not to use them otherwise.

'Not about quitting for good'

The idea follows similar initiatives aimed at abstaining from other activities, for example 'Dry January', when people avoid drinking alcohol, and 'Stoptober', when smokers try to quit.

As many as 320,000 people in the UK are thought to be planning to take part, according to a public poll by the RSPH.

Their survey also found more than a third (34 per cent) of the public thought taking part would have a positive impact on them personally, rising to almost two-thirds (63 per cent) of 18- to 24-year-olds.

Shirley Cramer, chief executive of RSPH, said: 'When used in the right way, social media can have a lot of real positives for mental health and well-being, including improving social connectivity and providing a source of emotional support.

'We want to harness and promote those positives, so Scroll Free September certainly isn't about quitting social media for good.'

Ms Cramer said the campaign was aimed at helping people recognise which aspects of social media may be having a more negative impact on well-being.

Once identified, users can then use that knowledge to establish a healthier, more balanced relationship with social media in the future.

Cutting out negative aspects

She added: 'Whether it's scrolling before bed stopping you sleeping, following aspirational and unattainable accounts denting your self-esteem, or the ever-presence of phones getting in the way of your face-to-face interactions with friends and family, Scroll Free September gives us all the opportunity to identify those negative elements and cut them out for good.'

Claire Murdoch, national director for mental health at NHS England, said the campaign was right to highlight concerns about the contribution of social media to mental health issues in younger people.

She said: 'A major ramp up of services will be needed to deal with the problems as part of the NHS long-term plan.

'We need to see concerted action, with everyone taking responsibility, including social media giants, so the NHS is not left to pick up the pieces of a mental health epidemic in the next generation.'

31 August 2018

⇨ The above information is reprinted with kind permission from iNews. Please visit www.inews.co.uk for further information.

Social media: six steps to take back control

An article from **The Conversation.**

THE CONVERSATION

By Monideepa Tarafdar, Professor of Information Technology, Lancaster University

We've heard a lot in recent months about the dark side of social media: excessive use to the point of addiction, lack of privacy, and data capture without informed consent. But in all of this melee, now is the time to remember that the way we use social media is up to us. In other words, it may be convenient to believe that social media applications are thrust upon us and we don't have much choice in the matter – but that is not entirely true.

It is time we remembered why we use these applications in the first place – to enrich our relationships – and not to have them take over our lives in a dysfunctional way. So, here are some tips for taking back control:

1. Be selective in your responses

Research shows that social overload – where your friends frequently ask you for advice on things such as restaurants in a new city, prom dresses for their kids, birthday cake recipes (pretty much anything really) – is stressful. Be selective about the posts you respond to. If a friend is posting 100 times a day you don't have to respond to all or any of them. Trust me, they won't mind, because anyone who is doing that amount of posting is not keeping tabs on who is responding anyway.

2. Stop worrying about missing out

You have no control over what gets displayed on your screen and when. The social media provider decides that. Which means you have no control over what you don't see either. Checking frequently is not going to change that – of all of the thousands of things your friends post, you have no idea what you will see and what you won't – so FOMO (fear of missing out) is pointless.

There will always be things you'll miss no matter how frequently you check.

3. Don't let it be a distraction

Don't let interruptions in the form of social media updates distract you. Though this can be easier said than done – because updates can happen anytime, while you are working, playing with your kids or, worse, driving. The dangers of such interruptions are well known – reduced attention, productivity and effectiveness at tasks. So make a choice, either don't let the notifications disrupt you or if you can't do that, turn them off.

4. Don't be fooled

Don't take everything you see on social media at face value. Research shows that people might experience all sorts of negative emotions – envy, worry, depression – when they see friends post pictures of where they've travelled, new houses they've bought and how well their children are doing. But it's important to understand that posts can be misleading because they present only partial views of other peoples' lives. Don't compare your 'behind-the-scenes' with everyone else's 'highlight reel'.

5. Set limits

Set time limits for how long you'll spend on your laptop, tablet or phone – even if you are doing other things on that device and are not using social media. While working on these devices, it is natural to take a break, but if you don't actually step away physically, then your break might consist of browsing social media and getting stuck in an endless cycle between work and social media.

Discipline yourself to get up every time you hit your limit, walk around, stretch, talk to someone, go into another room to see what the kids are doing, go to the office water cooler to get a drink – anything. This not only gives you a break from whatever you were doing to replenish your energy, it also prevents you from looking at your social media applications as the predominant alternative to work-related tasks.

6. Remember reality

Finally, actively seek ways to interact with your friends away from social media – meet up in person or call them. Social media is fine for sharing pictures and brief updates, but when you want to share the really important things in your life with those you care about, there is hardly a substitute for hearing their voice or looking into their eyes.

Human empathy – the kind that forms the bulwark of a meaningful social life – is very hard to convey through mass posts and text-based responses. A lot is lost between you and your friends when social media is the primary or only means of communication. Going for a walk or a run, having a meal, watching a movie, talking about your job and your kids, seeking support in difficult life situations – all of these things (and more) are what make your friendships warm and alive and real.

4 May 2018

Break away from phone addiction with this simple trick

Nip your phone addiction in the bud.

By Sabrina Barr

We're all guilty of checking our phones far more than we need to, whether we're incessantly refreshing our Instagram feed during the morning commute or getting the lowdown on the latest viral memes on Twitter.

More than two-thirds of people in the UK would confess that they use their phones too often, as noted by a survey conducted by Deloitte last year.

While many of us would admit that limiting phone use is far easier said than done, there is a simple trick that you can try in order to become more conscious of the amount of time spent mindlessly checking your phone.

Earlier this month, lead digital education correspondent for NPR and author of *The Art of Screen Time*, Anya Kamenetz appeared on the TiLT Parenting Podcast to discuss the way in which parents use their phones in front of their children.

She recommended that parents try announcing what they're doing when they check their phones. Doing this would help them create an open environment with their children while also enabling them to become more aware of their actions.

'What's helpful for me is something that my friend Danah Boyd, who's a social media expert suggested, and that is when you pick up your phone around your kids, simply narrate what it is that you're going to do,' she said.

'So you say, 'Hey, let's check the weather', or 'I'm wondering if dad has come home from work, I'm going to send him a text' and making that transparent.

'I think it is a really wonderful way to hold yourself accountable too, and to help kids understand what it is that you're doing.

'At the same time, you're not going to pick up your phone and look at your kid and say, 'Oh, I want to see what Rihanna's up to on Instagram.'

If this method doesn't float your boat, then there are other techniques that you could utilise to take control of your phone addiction.

Catherine Price, author of *How to Break Up With Your Phone*, advises establishing phone-free periods during the day, gradually building up from 30-minute breaks to a full 24-hour digital detox.

Spending too much time on your phone can drastically affect your productivity on a daily basis.

'The University of California found that if we get distracted from a task by a mobile phone notification, it takes us an average of 23 minutes and 15 seconds to fully regain our focus. All of which suggests that smartphones, while fundamental to day-to-day life, are detrimental when it comes to being productive,' explains Maths Mathisen, CEO and co-founder of Hold, an app that rewards students for putting down their smartphones.

'By not having your phone on, or in front of you, you minimise the amount of distractions around you, allowing you to focus on your work,' Mathisen advises.

22 February 2018

Key facts

- 99 per cent of people aged 16–24 in the UK in 2016 said they had used social media within the past week. (page 1)

- 63% of the UK uses social media every single day. (page 3)

- 77% of the UK are accessing social networks each week; 4.8 different platforms are used on a weekly basis. (page 3)

- 22% of daily mobile phone usage amongst those under 21 is spent with social media. (page 3)

- 17% of people owned a smartphone a decade ago. That has now reached 78%, and 95% among 16-24-year-olds. (page 4)

- People in the UK now check their smartphones, on average, every 12 minutes of the waking day. (page 4)

- Two-thirds of adults (64%) say the Internet is an essential part of their life. (page 4)

- Two-fifths of people (41%) say being online enables them to work more flexibly, and three-quarters (74%) say it keeps them close to friends and family. (page 4)

- Half of all adults (50%) say their life would be boring if they could not access the Internet. (page 4)

- The average amount of time spent online on a smartphone is two hours 28 minutes a day. This rises to three hours 14 minutes among 18-24s. (page 4)

- The average person now has 7.6 active social media accounts, with 98% of people having at least one social network account. (page 6)

- Facebook Messenger and WhatsApp are used by over 50% of Internet users. (page 6)

- More than 11 million young people have fled Facebook since 2011. (page 7)

- 82 per cent of people aged 18 to 29 said that they do use Facebook. (page 7)

- 48 per cent of Internet users over the age of 65 use Facebook. (page 8)

- In 2015, Facebook earned almost US$18 billion, virtually all of it from advertising. (page 9)

- Men aged 25 and under use devices such as mobile phones, tablets, e-readers and laptops the most. Device use occupied 35% of their leisure time, whereas for women it was 29%. (page 11)

- Of all leisure time spent using a device, 46% of this time is spent alone compared with 29% without a device. (page 11)

- One in ten teenagers who reported being on social media had spent upwards of three hours a day online, though the average time spent was one hour 21 minutes per day. (page 12)

- Just 40% did homework on an average weekday. Boys were significantly less likely to than their female peers – 35 per cent of boys compared to 44 per cent of girls. Those who did do homework, spent an average of one hour 13 minutes doing it. (page 12)

- Almost a third of participants (32%) claimed to use social networking sites 'a great deal' every day. (page 15)

- Those at high risk of addiction used significantly more social media platforms. (page 15)

- Over the past ten years, there has been a 20% rise in the proportion of 16- to 24-year-olds who are teetotal. (page 16)

- One survey of plastic surgeons found 55 per cent last year reported seeing patients who wanted to improve their appearance in selfies. (page 17)

- Facebook expecting its largest growth of new members joining the platform in the UK to be among the over-55s users this year (a predicted 500,000, in fact). (page 18)

- 40% of mothers and 32% of fathers have admitted to having some sort of phone addiction. (page 18)

- 15 million UK Internet users (around 34% of all Internet users) have tried a 'digital detox'. (page 19)

- Most social networking sites stipulate a minimum user age of 13. (page 24)

- 91% of 16–24-year-olds use the Internet for social networking. (page 25)

- Social media use is linked with increased rates of anxiety, depression and poor sleep. (page 25)

- The average Facebook user can see into the lives of 338 friends. (page 29)

- Nearly all (99.9%) of the participating adolescents reported spending time using at least one type of digital technology on a daily basis. (page 31)

- Research has shown that 80% of victims of cyberbullying were also bullied face to face. (page 32)

- 24% of children and young people will experience some form of cyberbullying. (page 32)

- 17% of children and young people will cyberbully others. (page 32)

- In a survey by Ditch the Label, 47% of young people have received nasty profile comments and 62% have been sent nasty private messages via smartphone apps. (page 33)

- 91% of people who reported cyberbullying said that no action was taken. (page 33)

- 65% would consider taking part in Scroll Free September. (page 36)

- More than two-thirds of people in the UK would confess that they use their phones too often. (page 39)

Glossary

Cyberbullying

Cyberbullying is when technology is used to harass, embarrass or threaten to hurt someone. A lot is done through social networking sites such as Facebook and Twitter. Bullying via mobile phones is also a form of cyberbullying. With the use of technology on the rise, there are more and more incidents of cyberbullying.

Digital detox

A period of time where a social networking user spends away from using social media. This is often to break the habit, or addiction that some experience from using social media. Some people will also try to avoid all forms of digital communication, such as email or instant messaging in this time too.

Digital footprint

The 'trail' a person leaves behind when they interact with the digital environment. This evidence left behind gives clues as to the person's existence, presence and identity. It also refers to what other people may say about you online, not just yourself: sometimes also referred to as your online presence.

Facebook

A social networking service that allows people to connect with their friends and family. Facebook acts as a platform to share your likes and interests, as well as photos, in order to stay in contact and keep up with others.

Hashtag (#)

The hashtag symbol (#) goes in front or a word or phrase to identify the topic of that message. This is commonly used on social networking sites, such as Twitter. On Twitter, when a hashtag rapidly becomes popular this is referred to as a 'trending topic'.

Instant messaging

This may include any form of messaging service that allows for delivery of messages to one or more recipients. These messages may be publicly broadcast or intended as private, but as electronic media, they may be released into a publicly viewable location by any of the participants (SMS, WhatsApp, iMessage).

Internet

A worldwide system of interlinked computers, all communicating with each other via phone lines, satellite links, wireless networks and cable systems.

Millennials

Often referred to as Generation Y, millennials are typically born between the early 1980's and the early 2000's. This generation is associated with a familiarity of digital technology, communications and media.

Social media

Media which are designed specifically for electronic communication. 'Social networking' websites allow users to interact using instant messaging, share information, photos and videos and ultimately create an online community. Examples include Facebook, LinkedIn and micro-blogging site Twitter.

Social media addiction

This addiction means spending an increasing amount of time on social media, taking time away from other daily tasks. Those that are addicted experience unpleasant feelings if they cannot access their social media for any period of time. It can also affect people's sleep, as they often wake during the night to check their social media accounts.

Social networking sites

A place online where people, usually with similar interests, hobbies or backgrounds, can build social networks and social relations together. Examples include websites such as Facebook, Twitter and Pinterest.

Troll/Troller/Trolling

Troll is Internet slang for someone who intentionally posts something online to provoke a reaction. The idea behind the trolling phenomenon is that it is about humour, mischief and, some argue, freedom of speech; it can be anything from a cheeky remark to a violent threat. However, sometimes these Internet pranks can be taken too far, such as a person who defaces an Internet tributes site, causing the victim's family further grief.

Twitter

An online social networking and micro-blogging website. This site allows a user to send and read 'tweets' (updates) which consist of up to 140-character text messages.

WhatsApp

An instant messaging app that is free to use, but is tied to your mobile phone number. You can also make voice calls, video calls and send images and documents.

Assignments

Brainstorming

⇨ In small groups, discuss what you know about social networking. Consider the following points:

  • What are the different types of social networks?

  • What are the different types of social media?

  • How many do you use on a daily basis?

  • What is a digital footprint?

⇨ In small groups, create a list of pros and cons for using social media.

⇨ In pairs, discuss the signs and symptoms of social media addiction. Feedback to your class.

⇨ In small groups, list as many social networking sites as you can think of. Are they broadcast or narrowcast sites?

Research

⇨ Do you know what your digital footprint is? Type your name into a search engine and see what information you can find about yourself. Has this changed the way you view Internet privacy/security?

⇨ Design a questionnaire that will evaluate how much time people spend on social media daily. Distribute the questionnaire to your classmates as well as friends and family. Create a report on your findings. Take in to account the differences between age groups and genders.

⇨ Do some research to find out about positive, unusual and innovative uses for social media. Write some notes and feedback to your class.

⇨ Do some research on the minimum user age that social media sites have. Which sites have the lowest and highest ages?

⇨ Design a questionnaire to evaluate how social media makes people feel. Then feedback to your class. Consider the following:

  • Pressure to reply to messages – as many people use 'read reciepts' on WhatsApp or iMessage you can often see that someone has read your message but not yet replied.

  • Pressure to complete a 'Snapchat Streak' – If you lose the streak do you lose a friendship? Is it important to validate a friendship?

  • FOMO – How does the fear of missing out affect people? Does this encourage them to carry on using social media?

Design

⇨ Design a social network app that would be suitable for children under 13 to use. Consider features such as security, privacy and parental controls.

⇨ Choose one of the articles from this book that does not have an illustration attached to it and create your own.

⇨ Design a leaflet with tips on how to digital detox.

⇨ Create a poster on how to deal with cyberbullying.

⇨ Create an infographic using one of the articles in this book.

Oral

⇨ Are social networking sites beneficial or can they be harmful? Debate this question as a class.

⇨ Read *How a Digital 5 A Day can help children lead healthy online lives* (page 23). In pairs, discuss how social networking can be used in a beneficial way.

⇨ In small groups, create a presentation that explains the concept of social media addiction. Your presentation should be aimed at 11-year-old pupils, and should offer advice on how to spot an addiction and how to deal with it.

⇨ In small groups, create a short radio advert that promotes 'Scroll Free September'.

⇨ As a class, debate the minimum age requirements that social networking sites stipulate. One half of the class should be against a minimum age, and the other in favour.

Reading/writing

⇨ Watch *The Circle* (2017) (12). How does this film portray the topic of social media? Do you think this is a realistic portrayal? Do you think that social media may develop this way in the future? Write a short story using the film and your thoughts on it as inspiration.

⇨ Imagine that you are an agony aunt/uncle and you have had a letter from a teen who is being cyberbullied. Write a reply to them telling them how they can get help. Read *What to do if you're being bullied on a social network* (page 33) to give you some ideas.

⇨ Read *Admit it, older people – you are addicted to your phones too* (page 18). Write an email to your parents/carers to try and persuade them to use social media less.

⇨ Read *Young people and social networking services* (page 24). Use this to write a blog on 'Keeping safe online'.

⇨ 'Children should be taught social networking skills at school.' Do you agree or disagree with this statement? Write 500 words exploring your answer.

addiction, to social media 13, 15–16, 18–19, 36, 38–9, 41
Amazon 5
antivirus software 21
Apple technology 5

body dysmorphic disorder (BDD), and social media 17
broadband 1
bullying, online 25, 32–5, 41

chat rooms 1
cloud computing 2
communication technology 4–5, 11
computer safety 20–5
Content Management Systems (CMS) 1
cyberbullying 25, 32–5, 41

Digital 5 A Day 23
digital
        dependency 4–5
        detox 19, 36–9, 41
        footprint 24, 27–8, 41
        wellbeing 14–15, 31–2

Facebook 1, 2, 3, 5, 10, 29, 41
        bullying and 33–5
        digital wellbeing tools 14–15
        Messenger 6, 7
        privacy and 21
        teen disengagement 7–9
fake news 3, 26
'fear of missing out' (FOMO) 15, 19
firewall 21
flexible working 5

gaming 12, 18
'gaming disorder' 19
gender, and social media 12
Generation Y 41
Google+ 2
Grindr 2
grooming, online 35

hashtags 34, 41
homework, and social media 12

Instagram 1, 2, 3, 5, 10, 18
instant messaging 1, 41
Internet 41
        chat rooms 1
        cloud computing 2
        dependency on 4–5
        mobile 2
        safety 20–5
        Web 2.0 1
        see also digital footprint; social media

leisure time, and social media 11
LinkedIn 1, 2, 8
location settings, social media 34

marketing, viral 2
mental health, and social media 13, 17, 19, 25–7, 29–32, 36–7

millennials 41
mobile Internet 2
multi-networking 6

Netflix 5

Ofcom, on communication technology 4, 19
online grooming 35

parents
        and Internet safety 20, 21
        and smartphone addiction 18
personal information, and social media 28
Personal, Social and Health Education (PSHE), and social media 26
Pinterest 1, 2
plastic surgery, and Snapchat 17
privacy, and social media 21, 24–5, 28, 34

Safer Internet Day 20
safety, online 20–5
screen time 14–15
Scroll Free September 36–7
smartphones 2, 4–5, 11
        addiction to 18, 39
        dependency on 4–5
Snapchat 1, 2, 3, 5, 7–8, 13
        plastic surgery and 17
        bullying and 33–5
        filters 17
        Snap Map 34
'Snapchat dysmorphia' 17
social media
        addiction to 13, 15–16, 18–19, 36, 38–9, 41
        and body dysmorphic disorder (BDD) 17
        closing accounts 35
        companies 2
        compulsive checking of 19
        definition 1, 41
        inappropriate behaviour 34–5
        location settings 34
        marketing 2, 3
        mental health and 13, 17, 19, 25–7, 29–32, 36–7
        minimum ages 24
        offensive content 24
        personal information 28
        unfriending/blocking 35
        use of 3, 6, 10, 28
        young people and 3, 4–5, 7–9, 11–15, 22–8, 31–2
        see also digital footprint
Social Media Day 3
Social Media Motivations Scale (SMMS) 10
social proof 19

'Technoference' 18
Tinder 2
trolling 41
		see also cyberbullying
Tumblr 2
Twitter 1, 2, 3, 5, 7, 19, 41
		bullying and 33–5

video games 12
viral marketing 2

Web 2.0 1
WhatsApp 5, 6, 19, 41
		bullying and 33–5
		privacy and 21

young people
		homework and 12
		social media and 3, 4–5, 7–9, 11–15, 22–8, 31–2
YouTube 2, 3, 5, 6
		bullying and 33, 35
		viral marketing 2

Acknowledgements

The publisher is grateful for permission to reproduce the material in this book. While every care has been taken to trace and acknowledge copyright, the publisher tenders its apology for any accidental infringement or where copyright has proved untraceable. The publisher would be pleased to come to a suitable arrangement in any such case with the rightful owner.

Images

All images courtesy of iStock except pages 2, 6, 14, 27, 32: Pixabay. 9, 11, 14, 18, 27, 29, 30, 32, 37, 39: Unsplash.

Icons

Icons on pages 4, 5, 22 were made by Freepik from www.flaticon.com.

Icons on pages 4, 5, 22 were made by Smashicons from www.flaticon.com

Icons on page 22 were made by dDara from www.flaticon.com

Illustrations

Don Hatcher: pages 6 & 31. Simon Kneebone: pages 12 & 34. Angelo Madrid: pages 10 & 21.

Additional acknowledgements

Page 31: Dr Andrew Przybylski, University of Oxford, www.ox.ac.uk/news/2017-01-13-'goldilocks-amount-screen-time'-might-be-good-teenagers'-wellbeing		[Accessed August 2018]

With thanks to the Independence team: Shelley Baldry, Danielle Lobban, Jackie Staines and Jan Sunderland.

Tina Brand

Cambridge, October 2018